The Decision

Odara's Rise (Book 3 of 3)

CARLA J. LAWSON

The Decision: Odara's Rise (Book 3 of 3)

Carla J. Lawson

© **2022**

All rights reserved. No portion of this book may be reproduced, photocopied, stored, or transmitted in any form except by prior approval of the author or the publisher, except as permitted by U.S. copyright law.

Published by CJL Books &
www.diverseskillscenter.com

Editing by Rothesia Stokes

Printed in the United States of America

U.S. Copyright No. 1-11127799167
ISBN: 978-1-7347924-4-7

Table of Contents

Dedication..4
Acknowledgements...5
Introduction..9

Chapter 1: The Council's Arrival 11
Chapter 2: The First Moon.. 45
Chapter 3: The Second Moon 65
Chapter 4: Older Odara's Plight 83
Chapter 5: The Third Moon 123
Chapter 6: The Fourth Moon 133
Chapter 7: The Fifth Moon......................................143
Chapter 8: The Decision..157

Contact Info..174

Dedication

This book is dedicated to my mother Jennifer Blackman Lawson, my father Samuel Eugene Lawson, my cousin Phillip Drake, my godfather Kenny Johnson, my mother of the heart Veatrice Davis, my cousin Valerie Atiah Hackett, my mentor Intisar Shareef, my godfather Roosevelt Weir, my mother's assistant Blanca Perdomo, my uncle Carlos Lawson, my cousin Cleave Lawson, my beautiful friend Kelly Ceballos and both of my grandmothers, Mae Evelyn Lawson and Bessie Blackman. May you all rest in heavenly bliss as I do the work that God put me here to do. I hope that I can touch and inspire people's lives as deeply as you did mine.

Acknowledgements

Throughout the course of writing "The Decision," the third and final book of the trilogy "Odara's Rise," the entire world entered a season of chaos and illness. In this book's beginning stages, my mother and best friend Jennifer Blackman transitioned from this world to heavenly rest. Finally, after a year of soul-shaking grief, I was able to manage the pain from that loss and begin writing again.

I would be remiss if I did not fully acknowledge the people who have supported my journey as an author who took on the task of entering the literary world with a trilogy. Their support has been unwavering and absolute.

First, I would like to thank my patron donors for the contributions that enabled me to have my books professionally edited, published, and presented in a manner worthy of their content. Regardless of what they gave, it all went towards a finished product that I am proud of, and hopefully, they are too.

Erma Smith, Linda Pinkney, Donna Collins, Tamie Griffin, Sharifah Freightman, Lillie Freightman, Greta Freightman, Tanisha Hodge, Ryan, and Jessica Cerami, Patsy Sherman, Karen Goodbar, Esther Campbell, Erma Smith, Kahila Nilsson, Arthur Roland Realty, Kenny and Alvin Pickettay-Jones, Corey Lawson, Judy Hall, Flossie Weir, Michelle Prior Alameda, Raymond Deshawn Hackett, Ola Lawson, Lester Jones, Regina Knight, Dwight Hilton, James Tobias and my incredible mother Jennifer Blackman.
Thank you from the bottom of my heart for your love, support, encouragement, appreciation, and donations.

What came to me in a dream that turned into a complete trilogy was brought to fruition courtesy of what you shared, gave, and poured into me. Your support means the world to me, and I will always cherish your contributions.

I would also like to give hearty, love-filled acknowledgments to Bruce and Sherisse Taylor for providing me with a safe, beautiful, peaceful place to complete this book. Lisa Mills, Donna Collins, Trevelyn Lee, and Greta, thank you for letting me scream, cry, check out completely, and show up with whatever strength I did or did not have throughout the illness and transition of my mother. Prentice Powell, whom I have never met but have followed for years via open mics, social media, and wherever else I saw your name. Thank you for inspiring a character that was critical to this trilogy. Your public growth, unapologetic transparency, and humility, along with your brilliance as an artist, literally provided me with the muse for the amazing warrior named after you in the trilogy. Salute!

Last but not least, Nicole Forrest, the friend who goes back to kindergarten, who showed up during my darkest hour and never left my side. The friend that saw my pain at its deepest, my clouds at its darkest, and my storm at its fullest. The friend who never judged erratic or illogical behavior came to see me physically for 355 days of the most challenging year of my life. I love you beyond measure for walking with me back into the light and for always seeing the good in me and claiming the best for me. Nu! Me and you, us never part! Thank you again, everyone; this is just the beginning! - Ms. Carla

Introduction

The Sacred Council was preparing to make a journey to the planet Earth. Odara, one of their finest spirit warriors had successfully completed her greatest assignment. The Council, Isis, Shango, Oya, Amaterasu, Bitol, Kali, and The Holy Trinity were pleased and proud of Odara and her ability to handle an assignment that not all of them agreed she would be able to. But she did. And in doing so, along with the help of her companion warrior Prentice, who traveled with her in the form of a black Persian cat, Odara had set in motion the restoration of balance in the planetary realm where Earth existed in the year 2019.

The arrival of the Sacred Council at Odara's current assigned home in the South of France during the Paris renaissance was not one she would be expecting. She also had no idea that she was up for promotion to the highest rank of spirit warrior. Odara would be presented with the opportunity to ascend to the level of warrior that no longer would carry out assignments in human form, nor in any planetary realm. She would assume her full spirit form and fight her battles in the spirit realm against the evils that constantly sought to sow discord and disrupt the progression and existence of the heavens.

Before she could do that, however, the Sacred Council would have to send her back through her time travels and assignments, back through the life of the body she lived in as Odara before she inhabited it, and through several realms and dimensions to gain a full understanding of who she was.

Once she did that, she would have completed the necessary steps to take full ascension. Then she would only have one thing left to do. Odara would have to choose between full ascension, which is only offered once to any spirit warrior, and not to all, or remain in the body of Odara until it expired, and it would be time to choose another human form. Odara was about to come face to face with the most important decision of her existence.

1
The Council's Arrival

Phillip sat patiently, waiting for the Sacred Council to give him the full details of his assignment with Odara. He was excited and proud at the same time. Throughout Odara's existence as a warrior from the spirit realm, he'd had the pleasure of watching her grow from a young, uncertain, inquisitive spirit unaware of her potential into a power-filled, wise, absolute warrior queen.

Odara and Phillip had an instant connection when they had to interact for the first time. She was a newly created spirit, a baby in the sentry for good. He was several centuries older than her when he was first called to bear witness to the work of Mutora, Roma, and Asir, the half-humans who were responsible for bringing her safely into a physical body that could withstand and endure a great deal. He remembered that her eyes were wide with wonder. Odara was always smiling, always ready to laugh, always joy filled and optimistic and always hungry to learn or try something new. When Phillip appeared to her for the first time, immaculately dressed and intrigued by the bell he had rung at the front door to Odara's home, she opened the heavy wooden door, looked him over from head to toe and giggled. "Welcome Phillip," Odara said as she moved from in front of the door to allow him to enter her home.

"How do you know who I am? I've yet to introduce myself." Phillip made no motion to enter the house as he awaited an answer to his question. Odara realized that he really was not going to move until she responded. She quickly got herself together mentally. The formality in Phillip's tone indicated that he was probably not one for word play or games.

"I was told to expect the messenger for the Sacred Council, and that I would know when he had arrived. Everything in my home settled and stopped when you rang the doorbell, so I knew you had to be Phillip."

Phillip smiled. "I'm glad to know that my arrival still commands order." He stepped into the front room of Odara's home and was pleasantly greeted by the scent of myrrh, fresh flowers, and what had to be something made from peaches coming from the direction of the kitchen. Phillip rememberedfondly that first encounter. He had provided herassignment, discussed at length the purpose of doorbells, and then enjoyed a cup of Earl Grey tea while tasting a small sample of peach cobbler, piping hot. He smiled at the simplicity and ease of their first conversation that turned into hours of time. Now, he was about to visit her again. The same wayhe always did when he had an assignment for her. The difference was that this time, he wasn't bringingan assignment. This visit would be the determining factor for if he would ever interact with Odara again.

Phillip never questioned the orders of the Sacred Council; he understood their purpose and his. He was just anxious to see if what he was assigned to do with Odara would help to make her decision process easier.

Isis, the Egyptian Goddess with magical powers greater than all other Egyptian Gods, was excited. She had a special affinity for Odara. She knew that Odara would struggle with what to choose when the options she was about to be presented with were placed in front of her. She also knew that she could not advise her beloved Odara in any way. She would have to sit back and wait for Odara to have her full preascension experience. What she could do, however, was provide Odara with a cushion for what she was going to see and must embrace. She felt that Odara was worth the explanation that she may have to give to the rest of the Sacred Council.

Isis called for Phillip. In an instant he was standing in front of his favorite member of the Sacred Council. In heavenly white robing, caramel-colored skin, and a clean shaved head; Phillip was aesthetically Godlike. Isis took note that he had been the messenger for the Council for so long that she wasn't quite sure how old he was. She spoke to him quickly. "Go to Odara and let her household know that the entire Council will be arriving soon behind you. I sense that you are concerned for her. You need not be, I'll be presenting an option to the rest of the Council before we arrive that will ease you and her both regarding what is about to happen. You will find out the details the same time that she does. Go now." Phillip nodded his head, took a bow and descended from the realm of the heavens towards the planet Earth to Odara's chateau in the South of France.

Odara and Prentice were seated on the patio at the chateau she had acquired as part of an assignment that had been diverted twice. They were both still reeling from everything that had transpired within the last forty-eight hours. Prentice was Odara's companion. A shape shifting black Persian cat that was sent to assist her in her work by the Sacred Council. Odara had learned through their experiences in her last assignment, that Prentice was so much more than just a shape shifter. He was some type of extraordinary being that hadn't fully revealed himself to her yet. She wasn't sure when that conversation would take place or if it even needed to. She was sure though, that she very well may not have survived her last assignment without him. Humble and appreciative, for now she just wanted to enjoy a great meal and laugh for a change. Prentice had assumed the form of a man for lunch's sake. A very handsome, well-dressed, milk chocolate-colored man with sparkling eyes and a beautiful smile. They sat patiently making small talk as they waited for Nicolette, one of the servants of the chateau to bring their beverages.

Prentice was enjoying the view of the orchard from the patio. The dining table outside was set with crisp white linens, gold flatware, crystal glasses, and an exquisite bouquet of purple roses and pink tulips. He could sense that Odara needed to rest. Her last assignment along with the events that followed once they arrived back at her chateau would have been enough to exhaust anyone – even a spirit warrior. The sound of the tribal drums that they had both heard before arriving to the chateau had not gone away. They had slowed some in pace, but he could hear them quite clearly still and was sure that Odara could too. What she couldn't hear that he could, was the sound of thunder, chimes, and the swooping sound of wings in flight. It was a combination of sounds that Prentice knew all too well. The Messenger was on his way, and right behind him was the Sacred Council. Prentice knew that something phenomenal was going down. Nicolette appeared tableside with a teapot and two tea settings. As she placed the settings on the table and poured their tea, Odara thanked her and asked about the timeframe for their meal.

Nicolette smiled and responded, "Lunch will be served within the next ten minutes, Mademoiselle." As Nicolette spoke, Prentice noticed that her eyes seemed to be almost glowing. As soon as he saw it, Nicolette looked at him with a smile. "A perfect day for lunch on the patio, is it not?" she asked.

Prentice looked into her eyes and sent her a message telepathically. "I see you, what in the world is going on?" Then he replied aloud, "It is most definitely a perfect day for lunch on the patio."

Seeing that Odara was oblivious to their exchange as she sipped her tea and admired the floral bouquet on the table, Nicolette responded to Prentice's question. "A lot, Prentice. For once I know something that you don't, after thousands of years. Today will be monumental. Enjoy your meal and keep Odara at ease, that is all we ask of you for now." Nicolette then winked at him and headed back to the kitchen to get their lunch.

Odara stood up and leaned over the table to smell the bouquet. As she inhaled the smell of the fresh flowers from her own yard, she made a mental note to show Prentice her sacred garden and maybe even her pantry. She had grown very fond of him and trusted everything about him. She thought about everything that had just happened in the last couple of days and wondered what his take on it was. "You heard Randall say that the man who commissioned his work was named Phillip, didn't you?"

Prentice took a sip of tea before answering her. "Yes, I did. And I heard him say that he was immaculately dressed and had impeccable manners. I also took note that he said the gentleman vanished without a trace." Prentice took another sip of his tea and was silent. Odara stared at him. She knew that he knew something, she could feel it. She also knew that he was blocking her in some ways, and she wanted to know why.

"Well, why would the messenger from the Sacred Council come to Paris, commission art that has images of things the artist knows nothing about and then leave?" Prentice was about to answer her when Nicolette appeared almost out of thin air with a rolling cart and several trays on it. Odara was annoyed and curious, but the smell of the food quickly dissipated her thoughts and questions. Nicolette removed the tray covers and placed their lunch in front of each of them. The chef had prepared croque monsieur sandwiches with frittes and a small garden salad. Odara was famished.

Prentice took her hand. "This looks delicious!" he said. "Let's have some wine as well." Nicolette looked at Odara who responded with "Perfect." A Petit Sirah, please, Nicolette," Odara requested. Nicolette nodded her head and was gone.

In between mouthfuls, Odara chattered about the splendor of the chateau, the landscaping, and the market in the nearest town. Prentice was glad she was preoccupied with her meal. He was incapable of lying and almost had to tell her about Phillip's visit to the artist being prophetic. Nicolette returned with a bottle of wine and poured them both full glasses. Odara raised her glass and said, "To friendship." Prentice toasted with her and took a sip of the wine. It was the perfect accompaniment to their meal. No sooner than he had gotten halfway through his glass of wine, Nicolette was back at the table removing their lunch dishes and pouring piping hot, fresh brewed coffee for them. Odara had fully relaxed.

The food, the wine, the view – it had all settled in on her. He looked at her as she sat back drinking her coffee. She was amazingly beautiful. She probably hadn't noticed that her face had matured and that her stature was stronger. As he watched her, he saw the wind swirling behind her at the same moment that she sat straight up and said, "Someone's here." They both turned towards the hallway and saw Giselle, the head servant for the home headed to the front door. As Giselle seemed to glide to the front door, the doorbell rang and Odara sat frozen as if she was fearful. Prentice took her hand again and they both stood up.

Giselle opened the door to Phillip standing there looking like a perfect picture in renaissance finery. A navy-blue waistcoat, grey trousers, blue and white striped vest, sparkling white shirt, yellow silk ascot, and a grey, velvet top hat; he was astonishing. Phillip removed his hat, placed it over his chest and greeted her. "Good afternoon, Giselle. It is a pleasure to see you again."

Giselle smiled and responded with a sweeping gesture of her arm. "Welcome Master Phillip. Please, come inside and I will let Mademoiselle Odara know that you are here."

As Phillip entered the foyer and stepped aside to wait for Odara, Giselle's mind went fondly to the memories of several encounters with Phillip. She walked away feeling deep love and devotion for him. Remembering that he was always only a message through the wind away when she was in the form of Mutora, she felt somewhat soothed that the Sacred Council chose to send him before their arrival. Odara was not expecting anything that was about to be presented to her, and him appearing first would give them time to set certain formalities in place; thus, giving Odara time to wrap her mind around the importance of their visit. Just as she was about to turn down the hall to head to the patio, Odara and Prentice were walking towards her already, hand in hand.

Giselle spoke first. "Master Phillip has arrived for a visit and is in the foyer, Mademoiselle Odara." Odara was both excited and afraid to see him. She was hoping that he was there to finally give her the assignment that accompanied her current living arrangements, but she was afraid that he may be there to summon her to see the Sacred Council. That summons could mean that they were not pleased with the results of her last assignment.

She shook off her worry and responded to Giselle. "Thank you, Giselle. Please bring tea to the drawing room for us. Phillip greatly enjoyed the Oolong tea during his last visit." "Of course, Mademoiselle," Giselle answered before heading to the kitchen.

Odara and Prentice walked into the foyer and Phillip was standing there as regal, patient, and breathtaking as ever. Phillip smiled from ear to ear when he saw Odara and opened his arms for a big hug. After releasing her from their embrace, he turned to Prentice. "An absolute pleasure to encounter you again, Prentice. I take it that you've embraced your new companion."

Prentice reached out and shook Phillips's hand. "I am most definitely in awe of the opportunity to share time and experiences with my new companion, Phillip. My last experience with companions didn't quite go so well." Phillip chuckled. "Oh, yes, yes indeed. That turned into quite a bit of a mess, didn't it?"

Odara had no idea what they were talking about, and really wasn't even interested. She was too anxious about the purpose of Phillip's visit to even ask questions. "Join us in the drawing room, Phillip. Giselle will have tea for us momentarily. I'm dying to find out the nature of your visit."

Prentice stepped ahead of Odara and opened the heavy, hand-carved solid wood doors to the drawing room. "After you, Odara." He stepped aside so that she could enter and then followed Phillip into the drawing room.

Odara took a seat in the large tufted purple velvet Queen Anne chair near the fireplace. Prentice sat down on the white brocade sofa directly across from her. They sat in silence as Phillip walked around the room. He moved slow and deliberately as he surveyed the oil paintings that now graced the walls of the drawing room.

Odara had questions for him, but he was so intently gazing at the artwork that she held her tongue. Phillip was blown away by the details and vibrancy of the paintings. When he commissioned Randall, a local young Black man who was selling his work on the streets of Paris, he was already aware that Randall had painted a stunning portrait of Odara. Randall of course, had no idea that he had been chosen because he would play a critical part in Odara's life when her next assignment was to take place.

Unfortunately, because of what was about to transpire, that assignment may never come to fruition. Depending on the outcome of the next few months events, another spirit warrior may have to take the place of Odara and see it through.

"Incredible talent and vision this Randall has, if I may say so," Phillip said. I gave him very few details with my requests. I did, however, plant a few seeds silently into his spirit. They seemed to have sprouted and took over during his creative process. I must admit that I am in awe of his work. Were you pleased when you received the series, Odara?"

Before she could answer, Giselle entered the room with a serving cart. Nicolette was right behind her. Phillip walked over and took a seat beside Prentice. "I understand that you enjoyed the Oolong tea from China during your last visit, Phillip?" Giselle said.

Phillip smiled at her and said, "Why yes, what a pleasant surprise to have the opportunity to enjoy it again."

Odara waited until the tea was served and was ready to answer Phillip's question and present her own questions. She noticed that after serving the tea, neither Giselle nor Nicolette stepped away to leave the room. As she was about to tell them thank you, she heard the wind swooping and swirling. It was loud and strong. It was also not coming from outdoors. She looked at Prentice and he was silently telling her everything would be fine. Simultaneously the sound of tribal drums began to fill the room. Low, but steady and rhythmic, they began to take over the airspace. Phillip set his tea down.

"Unfortunately, we don't have time to address events from the recent past. I am here because the entire Sacred Council will be here shortly. It is not a social call. You, Odara, have once again surpassed all expectations of the Council.

It is with great pleasure and honor that I am here to bear witness to their acknowledgement of your service and the offer that you will be presented with. In the interest of time, I will cease with small details. I need to prepare this space for their arrival which will be soon. Everyone in this room will need to assume their natural form and you will receive them as the spirit you were created to be. Your physical form will be shrouded and protected from the power of their presence until they have concluded their visit."

Odara's mouth dropped open. She was caught off guard and overwhelmed by the thought of the Sacred Council coming to her home. She was aboutto ask a question when Phillip spread both of his arms out and transformed himself. Now cloaked in an emerald green ceremonial robe and draped in gold tribal jewelry, he reached into his cloak and produced a small sphere. In one motion Giselle retrieved the sphere from him and took a step towards Odara. Odara sat in amazement as Giselle and Nicolette joined hands and returned to the physical forms of Mutora and Roma. They were both in white linen gowns heavily embroidered in gold. Giselle's neatly braided and bound hair now fell freely from her head as Mutora; a silver magnificent crown of natural curls, full and lively.

Nicolette was taller and younger than Giselle. When they transformed, her gown fit her body like a glove, and as Roma, she donned a cornrowed crown of hair that fell down her back with cowrie shells and gold beads threaded throughout. Odara sat blinking, everything was happening so quickly. She tried to stand, and Phillip raised his hand. She was immediately rooted to her seat. She actually could not stand up on her feet. She looked up at Phillip in bewilderment and then Prentice stood up.

Odara was completely unprepared for what happened next. As Prentice stood up, Phillip, Mutora, and Roma all dropped to one knee. They were showing reverence! What in the world is going on and who in the hell is Prentice? She looked at all three of them on one knee with their heads bowed and then looked up at Prentice. He smiled at her and then a blinding light filled the room. When Odara was able to see clear she almost fainted. Prentice stood before her almost eight feet tall. His milk chocolate-colored skin was illuminated, and his body was perfectly chiseled. He had a large bun of braided hair in the back of his head, and he was draped from the waist in an orange sarong that went to the floor.

Odara stared at the magnitude of the muscles in his arms and chest and then he dropped his head, clasped his hands behind his back, and several sets of magnificent gold and white wings raised from behind him. They were full and almost touched the twenty-foot ceiling. Odara blinked back tears as he raised his head. Phillip, Mutora, and Roma regained their composure and stood up next to him, and they all looked at her with love in their eyes. Odara had no words. Prentice smiled at her while Mutora and Roma walked over to her. "Your questions are coming from the inquisitive human side of you. Connect with your spirit, we don't have much time." Mutora spoke to Odara softly.

Odara looked at the woman who was her first earthly parent and then back at Prentice who hadn't moved an inch or blinked as he stared at her. Then she looked him in the eyes and raised her voice. "Who are you, Prentice?"

Prentice realized that Odara was in shock. He had empathy for her reaction to everything that was happening in the room almost in the blink of an eye. He lowered his wings and walked over to her. Mutora and Roma immediately moved aside so that he could kneel and address her.

"I am all things at all times, Odara. I was created specifically to be a supreme angel. There is little I cannot do or do not know. There are no dimensions nor realms that I haven't entered, either for warfare, protection, or visit. There are only two angels more gifted than myself. I have been in existence since before the Council was created. Thus, even the Sacred Council is not certain of the full magnitude of my capabilities.

I was assigned to accompany and protect you at all costs. I serve them, just like you, for the greater good of the universe, loyally and faithfully, without question." Odara looked into the eyes of her companion/friend. She knew that the form of a black Persian cat was just a shell for him, but she had no idea that he was who he was now saying he was. She had heard of the supreme angels and their powers and gifts. She just never thought she should have reason to meet one of them, let alone be assigned one as her companion. She didn't even want to think about what she may have to encounter that would require this level of protection. Prentice took her hand and kissed it. "You are not even aware of who you are yet, Odara. I am honored to be here for you." Then Prentice stood and stepped back. Phillip spoke sternly. "I still need to prepare this space."

With that statement, Mutora stepped forward and produced the orb that Phillip had handed to her when he first transformed. Flanking Odara on both sides, Mutora and Roma faced her. They raised their hands over her head and Phillip raised his left hand towards Odara. They spoke in unison. "Unsahlleba, swanegghabash, tosidious, magneyatta!

Relinquish the body you reside in and show yourself. Be here now, Machaneka, in full power and form!" As they spoke in ancient tongue, the orb began to magnify in size and Odara felt herself being pulled. Her eyes rolled back in her head and her body fainted as she realized she had no control overwhat was happening. Her spirit took over as she was released from the body that she had become so fond of. She stood in front of Prentice in her full spirit form as Mutora and Roma encapsulated her physical body in the orb and then sealed it. It was amazing to see the body she had been residing in lay out in the orb as if in a deep comfortable sleep. Mutora and Roma guided the orb towards the door of the drawing room. They exited, heading upstairs to Odara's bedroom to place her there until the Sacred Council was gone.

Mutora and Roma walked in unison side by side in front of the orb that held Odara's physical body. They were both very proud of her. When they were called by the Sacred Council to assist her as house servants, in the forms of Giselle and Nicolette, they knew that there had to be a reason other than familiarity. The night before Odara had returned to the chateau, as they were preparing for bed, they both heard the drums of the Council. Joining one another in the hallway and then following the drums onto the balcony in Odara's bedroom, they were thrilled when her sacred garden sprouted in full bloom as the instructions from the Sacred Council filled the night sky. When the message began to dissipate, the garden began to retreat, and they stood like proud parents looking at one another in astonishment. Neither of them spoke a word. They just returned to their sleeping quarters and went to bed.

Just a couple of days later, Mutora and Roma were guiding Odara's body to her magnificent boudoir to be wrapped for preservation. Upon approaching the bedroom door, Mutora commanded the door to open and they entered without having to stop or miss a step. They guided the orb to the center of Odara's bed and then joined hands over it. When they released their hands, the orb lowered, and Odara's body lay in the center of the bed amidst the large purple, gold, orange, and pink velvet throw pillows that she loved. Once her body was in resting position, Mutora and Roma took position at the head and foot of the bed. Mutora pulled a thread of light from the orb and Roma did the same from where she stood near Odara's feet.

They looked at one another and then issued aloud the command, "Rise!" Odara's body lifted a few inches from the bed. Mutora working from Odara's head and Roma working from Odara's feet began to wrap the thread of light around Odara's body until they met in the center of her body just above her womb. When they met in the center, they crisscrossed the thread of light and switched places, continuing to wrap the light around her until they both were in the opposite position from where they began. Once again Mutora and Roma made eye contact and then issued the command, "Release!" Odara's physical body lowered onto the gold, plush quilted blanket that covered her bed and was completely still. She was now enshrouded by light and the preservation process was almost complete. Roma lit the seven white candles that were on Odara's dresser and then joined Mutora at the foot of the bed. They turned so that they were back-to-back and spread their arms out so that they were outstretched toward all four corners of the room.

Mutora then called for more protection. "On behalf of the Sacred Council, we call for five senior guardians to assume position in all four corners of and at the door to this room. Our beloved will be rendered into your care until her destiny has been accepted and agreed upon. No one shall enter this room until the Council orders us to release the seal that will be placed upon it.

Because we are incapable of digesting the sight of you, when I feel your presence, we will leave this room and the seal shall be set. Please join us now."

Mutora and Roma lowered their arms and bowed their heads. Swirls of light began to enter the room and circle as they waited. The light swirls encircled Odara's body and continued to spin above her for a few moments. They joined until a large glow covered the entire bed and then split at once, four of them, each taking a corner of the room. The fifth one, considerably larger than the other four, hovered in front of the bedroom doorway and then the light from the swirls was gone. Mutora and Roma turned and walked to the bedroom door to leave the room. Standing in the doorway with her back still turned

Mutora spoke again. "Thank you for your presence and your protection." She and Roma walked out of the bedroom and closed the door. Once the door was closed, they heard many feathers ruffling. Roma smiled at Mutora and they began walking back down the hall to go downstairs and rejoin the others in the drawing room.

Downstairs in the drawing room, Prentice was taking in the majestic presence of Odara in her spirit form. The beautiful woman that she was in a physical body was amplified and multiplied in the spirit. Now as Machaneka, she stood before him tall and regal. The orange and gold fitted gown that covered her body seemed to be alive with the fire that she was created from. A foot and a half of natural curls sprang from her head adorned with gold threads pulled through them. A gold disc sat inthe middle of her forehead with a flame engraved init. An emerald amulet hung from her neck and her wrists were covered with several sets of jeweled bangles. Her skin was the color of a deeply bronzed statue. Her eyes sparkled and twinkled as she watched him taking in her presence. She felt incredible. It had been several centuries since she had assumed spirit form for something other than defense for battle. Just as Prentice was admiring her, she was mesmerized by his true form. She felt a connection with him that she had not felt while in her human body. It was deep and strong. They stared at each other in silence and then Phillip stepped in between them. "While this is quite captivating, there are only a few moments left for me to prepare this room for the Council's arrival. Please relinquish this hold you have placed on one another so that I can continue with what I am here for."

Prentice looked at Phillip and then stepped back. "As you wish, Phillip."

Odara, now as Machaneka, settled herself and stepped back as well. "Yes, sir," she replied. Phillip walked to the center of the room just as Mutora and Roma were returning to join them.

Mutora and Roma entered the room and then stopped to a complete halt. This was the first time since they had worked together to bring Machaneka to life that they had ever seen her in spirit form. They had known of her physical forms plenty of times, and even had become quite fond of her as Odara, but seeing her in full spirit presence was breathtaking. Roma reached for Mutora's hand, and they stood proudly, hand in hand, absorbing the beauty and power that she radiated. Machaneka smiled and bowed her head to them. They returned thesentiment and then Phillip took over.

"Let everything in this space now be suitable for heavenly accommodation. Let nothing be remiss of said accommodation. From the wood of the floors to the marble of the fireplace mantle, from the drapes in the windows to the pictures on the walls, all furniture, all accoutrements, and every inch of air space. This space is now commanded to be Holy ground. Anything tainted in this space whether it be person, spirit, or material thing will now be removed by order of the Sacred Council.

As the wind cleanses and the fire consumes anything unworthy of Holy presence, let this space commence preparation for the arrival of the Sacred Council."

As soon as Phillip finished with his command the room came to life. The walls and ceiling seemed to evaporate as winds with hurricane force filled the room. Phillip, Mutora, Roma, Machaneka, and Prentice stood side by side as the wind spun and dived then began to settle.

When it had come to a complete halt, a burst of flame erupted in the middle of the room. Prisms of light flew forth from the flame and went in every direction. Nothing in the room was untouched. As the last prism flew out and reached the ceiling, all the other prisms returned to the flame they had come from. The final prism spread light across the entire ceiling and then returned to the flame that extinguished itself.

The drawing room in the chateau was now cleansed and prepared for the Sacred Council's arrival. Everything in it sparkled and gleamed. The furniture itself even appeared to be new, almost alive with energy. Phillip held his hands out from both sides of his body and then spoke to everyone. "Join together, everyone, please." They each extended a hand to one another until they had formed a circle.

"Let each one of us welcome the Sacred Council through identification. I will go first. As the messenger for the Sacred Council: I, Phillip, esteemed and humble servant, welcome the Sacred Council into this space."

Mutora was next. "As an assigned lightworker and healer for the Sacred Council: I, Mutora, honored and humble servant, welcome the Sacred Council into this space." Roma followed Mutora. "As an assigned lightworker and keeper of life secrets for the Sacred Council: I, Roma, lovingly and humbly welcome the Sacred Council into this space."

Prentice followed Roma. "As an angel of the elite sentry, formed before the Sacred Council by the previous Council: I, Prentice, willing and devoted servant to all Councils for the greater good of all time, graciously welcome the Sacred Council into this space."

Last to speak was Machaneka. "As a spirit warrior of the second sentry for the Sacred Council: I, Machaneka, respectfully and humbly welcome the Sacred Council into this space."

After Machaneka spoke, they remained joined together by hands in stillness and quiet. Phillip raised his head up and spoke. "We are fully prepared for your arrival!" They all took a step back from one another and the sound of tribal drums filled the room. Machaneka felt the presence of relief. As Odara, she had wondered if she had failed her last assignment. She had been concerned that the Sacred Council would summon her in a state of disappointment. Her concerns were now being erased. The tribal drums that filled the room were beating in celebratory fashion. That meant that whatever business was about to take place, it had nothing to do with disciplinary action or disappointment. Excitedly now as Machaneka, the name given to her spirit and first physical body, she couldn't wait to see what was about to happen. The wait was less than momentary.

The drumming ceased and divine light shone down in three parts of the room and then joined to become one. As the parts of light became one, the form of a middle-aged man with bronzed skin and a mane of tightly curled hair stood before them. He wore a white and gold robe that covered him completely. He stood with a smile on his face as the room was filled with the overwhelming presence of absolute love and divinity. The Holy Trinity was the first to arrive, presenting itself in singular form for the purposes of this meeting. The love that the Holy Trinity was radiating from one entity was so powerful that it was almost tangible.

Machaneka was completely enthralled by what she was feeling when the sound of chimes blowing in the wind entered the room. In less than an instant sunlight flooded the space, and standing next to the Holy Trinity was Amaterasu, the Japanese Sun Goddess. She was heavily robed in a white kimono with red trim, exquisite gold jewelry, and a gold headdress.

Amaterasu majestically looked around the room and nodded her head in acknowledgement of everyone then folded her hands in front of her. Before anyone could move or blink, drums and chanting now took over the room and then stopped with one loud beat of a drum. Bitol, Mayan God of the sky, stood in the center of the room. Standing at six and a half feet tall, he wore a deep blue sarong and tribal body paint on his muscular body. He had gold and turquoise cuffs on his arms and legs, and a large, beaded necklace hung from his neck with a jade amulet. On his head, a large, plumed headdress with white, green, and blue feathers stood almost another foot tall. Bitol exuded strength and power. He turned and looked at Machaneka, smiled at her, then stood patiently next to Amaterasu.

As each entity joined them all, the drawing room seemed to get bigger. The arrival of the first three Council members had set the tone for the rest of them. The air was charged with energy and authority. Time seemed to have stood still momentarily. That moment erupted when a melody of finger cymbals graced the room. With no haste, Kali, the Hindu Goddess of time, doomsday, and death joined the other present members of the Sacred Council. Kali arrived in full Goddess splendor; jeweled, draped, and crowned. With pale blue skin gleaming in the light of the room, her wavy jet-black hair hung down to her waist. Wearing a necklace of shrunken skulls and barefoot, she raised all ten of her heavily gold ornamented arms and took position next to Bitol who almost looked amused. Kali said nothing. She was not one for salutations or idle chatter. The depth of seriousness to her charge as a Goddess hovered in the air around her. Machaneka almost trembled. Kali's appearance was definitely one that could shake anyone. That was until you saw the kindness in her eyes. While staring at Kali, who was not looking at anyone in particular but staring straight ahead, the ominous sound of great thunder shook the chateau.

Phillip looked up towards the ceiling and said, "Every time." Machaneka, Mutora, and Roma all had bewildered expressions. Prentice chuckled aloud. "I see you've never had the pleasure of this particular arrival."

Before Mutora could ask who it was, a lightning bolt came through the ceiling amidst the mighty roar of thunder, and standing in the spot where it hit the floor were Shango, Yoruba God of thunder and his wife Oya, Yoruba Goddess of thunder, lightning, tornados, winds, rainstorms and hurricanes. They were quite the duo. Oya's wine red flowing dress and Shango's red sarong, Oya's long coiled dreadlocks and Shango's mountain of braids, Oya's belt of nine pieces of children's clothing, and Shango's cowrie shell belt. It was a royal sight that was finished with the gold ornamented headpieces they both wore that had beads hanging down over their faces as far as their noses. Oya waved her hand and the lightning bolt disappeared, leaving the strong, fresh scent of sandalwood and patchouli.

Shango took his wife by the hand, covered his chest with his other hand and nodded at Machaneka.

She smiled back at him, stunned and amazed by the beauty of them both when they heard the cry of an eagle. All heads turned in the direction of the sound and even Prentice gasped when wings that seemed to go through the ceiling appeared, spread, and then folded. When they unfolded, the last member of the Sacred Council stood before them radiating light: The Egyptian Goddess of life and magic who protected women and children and healed the sick. One of the most powerful Goddesses of all time, Isis had arrived.

Dressed in a gold fitted gown and jeweled Egyptian collar and cuffs, also wearing a gold headdress that fell to her shoulders with an obelisk in the center of the crown, Isis was the perfectpicture of a Goddess. She looked at everyone in theroom, and with a smile and a nod acknowledged each of them individually. When she got toMachaneka, she spoke in a quiet voice.

"My dearest Machaneka, I am proud to be here to address you in spirit form today.

You are so much more than the body that you have assumed as Odara. In you, young warrior, I am well pleased." Then she turned to Phillip, Mutora, and Roma. "Thank you for proper preparation of this space. Once again, Phillip, you have left no stone unturned. Mutora, I trust that Odara's body is fully protected and covered?"

Mutora and Roma answered in unison. "Our beloved Odara is fully covered and protected. We also called on five guardian angels to ensure that her time at rest will not be disrupted."

Isis smiled. "Well done." Turning to face the rest of the Sacred Council, Isis then took a small velvet bag out of her bosom. She opened it and poured its powdered contents into her hand. She held her hand up to her face and then blew it into the air. The small, powdered particles flew into the air, sparkling like miniature fireflies and then hovered in front of her. She stepped into it and commanded, "Seal this room!" and clapped her hands. The powder spread to the ceiling and continued to expand until the entire ceiling, every wall and doorway, had a sheer sparkling covering. It was now time for them to let Machaneka know why they were in Odara's chateau to see her.

Amaterasu was the first to speak once the room was sealed. "I was unsure of your future when you forgot the protective robing that I provided for you during a previous assignment. That oversight almost cost you the physical body that you inhabit as Odara. I was pleased when you not only completed that assignment but also contained the evil that was the catalyst for it.

You exceeded my expectations. It is with great pride that I and the rest of the Sacred Council are here to offer you the highest promotion that any spirit warrior can receive. To take full ascension as a spirit warrior."

Machaneka was unable to speak. What she was hearing was something she had least expected.

Prentice stepped up behind her for support. Then Kali spoke to her. "You have mastered your usage of time, the ability to promote balance through necessary death, and you have shown great fearlessness in battle. I am exceptionally proud of you for not having called for my assistance when there was something that you could handle yourself."

Bitol took a couple of steps closer to Machaneka and then addressed her. "Understand that this offer is only offered once to any spirit warrior who is deemed worthy. That if you accept this promotion, you will never again assume human form to fight for the greater good of the universe.

The body you have become fond of and accustomed to as Odara will continue to live a normal human existence, but you will have no connection to her. The realm that you will be assigned to reside in and protect will be determined if you accept this promotion, and once it has been accepted, there will be no turning back."

When Bitol finished his last sentence, Oya walked over to Machaneka and took both of her hands in hers. Looking directly into her eyes she spoke to her softly. "You have excelled time and time again for several centuries in everything that you did.

We questioned sometimes your capacity to fulfill assignments because you are very special.

You are one of the few spirit warriors who responds to some situations from emotion. While that could potentially be problematic, it has in your case proven to be an asset. I believe that you deserve without question this promotion. We have decided to not demand an answer immediately. The Council believes that there is a critical journey that you need to take before you respond to our offer. We need you to be absolutely certain when you come back to us about your decision."

Machaneka locked in a gaze with the beautiful, mystifying Oya, did not know what to say. She was trying to take it all in, listening intently and processing at the same time. She was shaken from her state of contemplation when the thunderous bass of Shango's voice addressed her. "I believe that you are capable but not ready for this promotion. I do not trust the attachment to your human form, Odara, nor do I trust your capacity to "feel" in a way that spirit warriors do not normally acquiesce to. I do appreciate your fearlessness, your tenacity, and your commitment.

Because of that and the favor of the other Council members, I am open to seeing how you handle your upcoming journeys and curious to see how they affect your decision."

Isis opened her arms and then hovered in the air. All of the members of the Sacred Council had spoken except for her and the Holy Trinity. Machaneka was overwhelmed but not afraid as her personal favorite from the Council started speaking to her in a strong, smooth voice.

"Before you make any decision you will be sent back to various places to bear witness again to things that contributed to who you are. You will see how the battles that you won and the one that you lost impacted the lives of those involved and the balance of the universe. You will see things that you have not had a single thought about once those assignments were finished. All of your travels will be in spirit form. The body of Odara that you normally inhabit will remain at rest, guarded, nourished, and protected by five guardian angels who will not move from their posts until they are released by my command.

You will encounter and see things through your spirit eyes that you may want to address, stop, or change. You are to do nothing regardless of any impending danger or strife to anyone. Your charge through this journey is only to see.

I am assigning Phillip and Prentice to accompany you. They will be your support and your protection, if necessary, even if that be from yourself. You will go where they take you without question and you will observe and sometimes relive moments from your past. This journey will run its course through five full moons. The first sunrise after the decline of the fifth full moon, you will return to this chateau and reassume the body of Odara. From that point you will have thirty earthly days to settle yourself between human and spirit. On the thirty-first day, Phillip will return for you to tell him what you have decided, and he will deliver your decision to us.

What happens after that depends on what your answer is." Isis paused, smiled at her, and then said, "Remember this, beloved Machaneka, there is no wrong answer."

Then the mighty wings that filled the room when she arrived spread out and up to the ceiling. Isis nodded at her, the wings closed around her like a cocoon, and she was gone.

Shango put his arms around his wife Oya and stomped his foot on the ground. A small funnel of clouds began to rise from the ground and envelop them, and then in the blink of an eye, they too were gone. Amaterasu sprang forward towards Machaneka. She reached inside of her robe and withdrew a small sunburst. She held it out for Machaneka to take it. "During your travels there will come a day when everything will be dark, and it will be troubling to you. Use this to brighten the atmosphere around you and soak up the power and hope of the light of the sun." Machaneka held her hand out and Amaterasu transferred the light from the sunburst to Machaneka. Before Machaneka could say thank you, the Sun goddess clasped her hands in front of her chest and was gone in a swirl of light.

Bitol and Kali stepped forward and Kali spoke in her deep, gravelly voice.

"Use the gift of time control that I gave you upon creation when you need to see without interruption. Only use it to see, not to control what is going on. Remember what Isis told you about not interfering with life as you will see it." Bitol raised his arms and said, "Return!" The sound of a rainforest filled the room and Bitol and Kali spun in a circle, and they too were gone.

The last member of the Sacred Council remaining in the room had been the first to arrive. The Holy Trinity in singular form. He motioned for Machaneka to come closer to him. When she was directly in front of him, he spoke to her with kindness, empathy, and love in his voice. "Are you accepting of the conditions of this journey as the basis for you to make a decision to be or not be promoted to the highest level of spirit warrior, assuming full ascension, Machaneka? And do you fully understand everything that was presented here today? And lastly are you prepared to be in spirit form with full power and not be able to do anything that alters the natural course of things that you may see, no matter how dire?" She looked at him with tears of humility in her eyes and responded, "Yes."

The Holy Trinity opened his arms and wrapped them around her in an embrace. "Then I gift you with an extra covering of patience, a double portion of understanding, and a well of wisdom." Machaneka felt the light and peace from the Holy Trinity flood through her. She felt as though she were airborne. It was a feeling like nothing she had ever experienced. He held her until she relaxed completely in his arms. "You are well covered, dear Machaneka. I bid you well until I see you again." The Holy Trinity released her from his embrace, put his hands behind his back, and vanished from her sight.

When she regained her composure, Machaneka looked around the room. Mutora and Roma had returned to their full human form, and they were standing there beaming with pride. They both curtsied to her and then left the room in a burst of squeals and excitement.

Prentice looked at Phillip and asked, "When is the first full moon?"

Phillip looked at Machaneka and replied, "Tonight." She inhaled, thankful that she wouldhave companionship, then she exhaled and said, "I am ready."

Just like the moon we go through phases

2
The First Moon

The drawing room was still full of powerful energy courtesy of the visit from the Sacred Council. Machaneka, still in spirit form was spinning from everything that had transpired. She sat down in lotus position to rest and let it all sink in. While she was doing so, Prentice knelt on one knee and bowed his head. She watched as his wings lowered then receded, and then disappeared altogether. When he stood again, he was considerably shorter but still at 6 feet 3 towering over her. Phillip raised his hands over his head then spread them out. In the blink of an eye he was no longer robed in ceremonial gear. Simply clad in full leg black pants, a white shirt, black shoes, and a grey and white men's kimono, he was quite striking. Machaneka laughed aloud. "Travel chic for you, Phillip?"

Phillip turned and looked at her. "I love the ease of clothes that move. I believe that this is one of my favorite travel ensembles."

Prentice was tickled as well. Knowing that they would all be in spirit form, he found it amusing that Phillip opted for regular clothing. He looked at Machaneka; she was radiating like a goddess, and he felt a sense of love, respect, and admiration. Prentice knew that the five-month season that was beginning that night would be very trying for her. He would do everything in his power to make it as comfortable and digestible as possible.

Machaneka stood and said, "I need to check on my body."

"Correction," Phillip replied. "You want to check on your body. Odara is in the hands of great care. But so be it. I know how attached you are to the physical vessel that you use. So does the Sacred Council. Hence, why you have been given the time that was allotted to make your decision."

Machaneka looked at him and Prentice and then stood. She bent over and drew a line across the floor with her finger and then stepped on it. "To Odara's bedroom!" Immediately she was encircled by a mist and then gone.

"I'm not sure how this is going to go, Phillip," Prentice said while still looking at the spot where Machaneka had been standing.

"It will go, Prentice, exactly like it is supposed to. Whatever happens, is what was meant to happen." Phillip sat down on the sofa, crossed his legs, folded his hands in his lap and then said, "She will be just fine."

Machaneka appeared in Odara's bedroom at the side of the bed where the body that she had occupied for a short period of time was perfectly bound and protected by divine light. The guardian angels who were responsible for Odara's protection stood at full salute at the sight of her. Wings raised, heads down, and hands clasped, they waited for her acknowledgement. Machaneka, in awe of the power of their presence, spoke aloud. "I would like to thank you for your protection and for your presence. Please be at ease, I will not be long." The angels lowered their wings and settled back into their corners.

A beautiful melody and the sound of a hymn being hummed quietly began to fill the room. Machaneka stood over the physical body of Odara and stared at her. She was completely enamored with the life that she had been experiencing in this body. She was also slightly tormented. For thousands of years, she had experienced hundreds of bodies.

She had been throughout the universe many times in battle and travels but never had she become attached to the body that she was inhabiting. Something about Odara was special, made her feel everything on a much deeper level. Something about her experiences as Odara made her want more of the human experience, made her desire to use her power through the vessel that was Odara. Machaneka smiled; there could be no physical contact because of the layered protection, so she just took a moment to admire Odara at complete peace and rest while the magnitude of her decision swam about in her mind. She hovered above her, stood beside her, watched her rest from the foot of the bed then finally after a couple of hours, Machaneka stepped back from the bed and the incredibly beautiful, intriguing body of Odara, and made her descent back to the drawing room where Phillip and Prentice were waiting for her.

When Machaneka reappeared in the drawing room, Phillip was standing in the window looking out over the courtyard of the chateau. The sun was beginning to set, and the room was filled with the pinkish golden glow of the sunset. Prentice saw that she appeared to be in deep contemplation, so he opted to wait a few minutes before mentioning that the time for them to leave was approaching. As Machaneka stood looking around the room she began to relax. She knew that shortly she, Prentice, and Phillip would be headed on a journey that could change everything about her existence. She was also excited to see where they would be going and what she was about to see that would be the determining factors for her decision to take full ascension as a spirit warrior or possibly not.

Prentice had joined Phillip at the window and the room began to dim as the sun and the moon exchanged places. Machaneka joined them and they all stood watching the sun retreat and the moon rise. Slowly they saw the beautiful exchange of powers from day to night and she took a deep breath as the night sky filled with the full moon. It was time to leave. Machaneka knew that she was ready. Phillip and Prentice both turned to face her. She looked them both in the eyes, raised her hands towards the window and then spoke. "The Sacred Council has preordered my journey. Transport us to the first destination now please."

In the blink of an eye, Machaneka, Phillip, and Prentice were swept up in a wind tunnel and then planted safely on the ground in front of a house where an 8-year-old girl was playing outside in her front yard. Machaneka felt tears forming as she was overwhelmed with an enormous flood of love filling her. Seeing the same thing that she saw and how she was reacting to the sight of the child, Phillip and Prentice spoke simultaneously. "Who is that, Machaneka?"

As she choked back tears, never taking her eyes off the animated, excited, brown skinned baby girl with puffball ponytails and ribbons in her hair playing alone in her front yard, Machaneka answered them. "Odara. That is my beloved Odara."

Phillip and Prentice stepped in closer to Machaneka to support her. She was almost hovering above the ground from the elation and the emotions that were taking over her. She never would have imagined that her first journey would be to see who Odara was as a child. To see the early stage of life for the body that she would later inhabit and come to adore. Eight-year-old Odara was oblivious to their presence of course. She sat on a blanket with four baby dolls positioned as if they were sitting too. In front of the dolls were plates and cups. Odara was opening a bag of potato chips and serving each of the dolls a small portion. As she shared her chips with each doll, she welcomed them by name to her picnic. She was so engrossed in setting up their lunch and talking to them that she did not see the three little girls about her age approaching the walkway to her yard. Machaneka watched intently. Prentice seemed to tense up slightly, and Phillip focused in on one of the little girls. Picking up on the two of them, Machaneka also changed her focus to the energy of the three girls. It did not feel good at all.

The tallest of the three brown skinned girls stepped onto the lawn and motioned for the other two to join her. She whispered to one of the other girls, "I told you she thinks she's better than us."

Odara looked up and saw the three girls standing there. "Hi! Do you want to have a picnic with us?"

Odara's question disarmed one of the girls who was about to step forward and say yes until the tallest girl answered quickly and harshly. "No! We don't play with people who think they're better than us. Showing off all of your dolls out here trying to make us jealous."

Odara answered her with kindness in her voice. "I have enough dolls for all of us to play, and I can get some more potato chips."

The two smaller girls looked at their friend and waited for her response. She gave it without much hesitation. "Stop getting smart. We do not want to play with you, and we do not like you. Nobody likes you. You think you're cute and you're not."

Machaneka saw that the girl was about to approach Odara, and she raised her hand. "No, you won't," Phillip said. "You have been instructed to observe, no matter what you see, no interactions."

Machaneka lowered her hand just as Odara was standing to her feet.

Odara was about three inches shorter than the girl doing the talking. She stood up and walked to the edge of the lawn where the girls stood. She put her hands on her hips and said, "I don't think I'm better than anybody, and I'm not showing off.

I'm playing with MY dolls in MY yard at MY house! I'm not ugly, I am cute, and if you didn't want to play with me why are you here?"

The two smaller girls stepped back, surprised at her boldness. The taller girl was taken aback. She realized quickly that she had lost some of her power over the other two girls and that she had to do something. She stepped closer to Odara and said, "What you gonna do? You're scared of me!"

Odara stood solid with her hands on her hips. "What I'm going to do is finish my picnic with my dolls in my yard at my house. What you're going to do is take your little friends and get out of my yard before something bad happens to you because I know magic, and I will put a spell on you, and you will wake up ugly and stinky."

Odara then closed her eyes and started chanting, "Ohmmmmm nommminaaa, Ohmmmm…" One of the smaller girls ran down the walkway and headed down the street. The other one stepped behind the taller girl.

The tall girl didn't know what to do. Odara was standing there with her eyes tightly closed getting louder and louder with her chant.

The next thing she did ended everything. Odara raised her hands to the sky and said, "I'm putting a spell on you nowwwww." The tall girl and the smaller girl took off running down the walkway.

Odara was still in deep chant, waving her arms and turning in circles when a voice from the front porch of her home asked, "Odara, what are you doing?"

Odara turned to see her mother Shamara standing on the porch of their home patiently awaiting an answer to her question. Odara ran to her and threw her arms around her waist. "Why do they hate me?" she asked. With tears streaming down her face, she buried her head into her mother's embrace. "I was putting a stink spell on them for being mean to me."

While concealing a giggle, Shamara looked down at her sweet baby girl who hadn't lived long enough to understand that some people will dislike you, just because you're you. She held her daughter for a moment and then lifted her face towards her with one hand. As she wiped Odara's tears she quietly began to speak to her. "First of all, I'm certain that they don't hate you, hate is a very strong word. Secondly, maybe they don't know how to make friends with someone as amazing as you, so they started off the wrong way. And lastly, as I've told you before, don't send bad thoughts about people out into the world. You will get back what you send out. Instead, when you say your prayers tonight before bed, you should pray for them to learn kindness."

Odara was sniffling now, her tears drying up as she thought about what her mother was saying. She looked up into her mother's face. "They were really mean, but I'll pray for them, Mama." Shamara smiled at her daughter and kissed her on her forehead. Odara stepped away from her and walked to the lawn to pick up her dolls and her picnic setup.

Phillip was smiling, Machaneka was slightly shaken and overwhelmed by the love that she felt coming from Shamara for Odara. Prentice hadn't moved an inch and had no expression on his face as he watched Shamara intently. Very intently. Just as Machaneka noticed how engrossed Prentice was with Shamara, a slight wind blew, and Shamara's gaze rose from watching Odara gather her things. She was looking in the direction that the three of them were watching from.

Actually, she appeared to be looking directly at them. Phillip went from smiling to looking alarmed. "Can she see us?!" he asked.

Machaneka now looking into Shamara's eyes said, "There's no way, can this be?" Prentice relaxed and answered them both. "No, she cannot see us, but she is gifted, and she knows there is a presence."

Shamara stared in their direction and whispered, "I know that you're here, and I know that you're here for Odara. I also know that one day, she will meet you."

The three of them stood in total silence side by side. "She is not of this place but definitely rooted here. Let us go now," Prentice said. Machaneka stepped into a swirl of wind with Prentice and Phillip and then stepped back out. She cupped her hands together and placed them over her heart then she opened them, and a beautiful orange and blue butterfly flew out of them towards Odara and Shamara. As she stepped back into the whirlwind to move ahead with Phillip and Prentice, she heard the words "thank you" float in her direction.

Back in the swirling wind with Prentice and Phillip ascending to their next destination, Machaneka closed her eyes for the transport. She opened them quickly after a few moments, realizing that all motion had stopped. Both of her escorts had joined hands with her between them. Phillip was sternly looking into her eyes. "You were instructed by the Sacred Council to only observe whatever you saw. You directly disobeyed the Council's order.

There will be repercussions for sure, they are watching your entire journey and your every move."

Machaneka lowered her head in shame. She turned to look at Prentice, hoping for a reprieve. He too had a stern, concerned look on his face. She turned back to face Phillip and addressed him. "I didn't interfere with anything or stop anything from

happening. What did I do that was so blatantly disrespectful?"

Without hesitation Phillip responded. "You sent a butterfly to them. And while Odara will only see a pretty butterfly that makes her smile, Shamara will know that her acknowledgement of our presence has been welcomed. It could possibly change the trajectory of her actions in the past, which would in turn change the trajectory of young Odara's journey, possibly altering the outcome of how her life turned out. Including but not limited to you assuming her body for your assignments. So be clear, you are to not to take ANY ACTION at all during our visits. Even a slight endearing one can end up being disastrous. I will send Prentice back to her to remove the memory for you this time. There cannot be another situation like this. If there is, I will consult with the Sacred Council on whether to cancel your travels with us or not. The inference from a second infraction of the only instruction would be that you are possibly not ready for the promotion that you were offered. Do you understand?"

Machaneka, now embarrassed for her carelessness and ashamed from being scoldedduring the most important time of her existence, held her head up and responded.

"Yes, Phillip, I understand. My apologies for the inappropriate action and my word on maintaining the integrity that I accepted this assignment with."

Phillip nodded at Prentice who was behind her locked by hands with him. They released their grasp of one another and then Prentice was gone from the transport.

Phillip spoke to her again. "We will have to navigate through the realm of transition to get to our next destination. You may possibly see things that are not pleasant. I need for you to fully embrace and embody the spirit warrior that you are. You are still too connected to human emotion for some of what you need to witness."

He did not wait for her to respond as he cloaked himself in all white for their travel through the realm of transition. Machaneka knew in her heart that he was questioning whether she was ready, and also that he was pulling for her to prevail. She did not want to disappoint him, and she did not want to return to face the Sacred Council as a failure. She raised her hands above her head, and using ancient tongue called for her covering. "Swahatilla Disodenus Yahsameha!" Phillip watched and waited patiently as the whirlwind opened and began to grace the spirit form known as Machaneka. The clouds dipped and swirled around her body almost lovingly as light shone over and through her entire presence.

They almost appeared to be delicately weaving the white shroud she needed for protection onto her body. Just as the swirls receded and her coverage was completed, Prentice reappeared next to them in the whirlwind. He nodded at Phillip and then looked at Machaneka. Before returning to join them from erasing the memory of contact from Shamara, he was slightly annoyed. But the sight of Machaneka, whom he fondly traveled with and assisted as Odara, was breathtaking. The celestial white covering that shrouded her was beyond beautiful. It was immaculate, sparkling with stardust and almost looked like several sets of fluttering wings opening and closing around her body.

He gathered himself as Phillip chuckled and Machaneka tried to understand the wonderment on his face. With an outstretch of his arms, Prentice was instantly covered in glowing white robing, fit only for the Spirit Realms finest as the whirlwind that was their vehicle through the realm of transition, cocooned them in a sheer veil to commence their travels.

Machaneka felt glorious. She had been so comfortable in Odara's body that she'd forgotten what it felt like to be fully free from worldly responsibility. The travel to and through different realms was completely different without an assignment that would probably end in battle attached to it. Her spirit mind was racing, she was honored and excited to have Phillip and Prentice accompany her. The whirlwind that was their transport felt like a luxury express elevator. She relaxed and looked at her escorts. They were both peacefully flanked by her sides and a strong sense of comfort overcame her. Phillip placed his hand on her shoulder and spoke softly. "We're almost at our next destination, you haven't even looked around at the beauty of the ascension realm." Machaneka opened her closed eyes and looked out past the whirlwind. She realized that as a spirit warrior she may never enter this realm again and she wanted to appreciate it. What she witnessed next did not disappoint her at all.

Incredible spheres and rays of light were everywhere. Inside of the spheres and gliding on the light rays were the spirits of people who had transitioned and were headed to the heavens. Machaneka took a deep breath as she saw the wonderment on the faces of those who were ascending. Some of them were obviously joyful and understood what was happening. There were others who were obviously still in a state of amazement and not quite clear what was happening. She saw people from all generations, from newborns who were smiling to the elderly who were standing tall knowing that they would arrive in the heavens and be restored to full strength. As she was taking in the beauty of it all she glanced at Prentice.

"Incredible, isn't it?" he said. "I'm thankful that this is the part of the realm that you are witnessing. The part that you weren't paying attention to is where those ascending haven't realized that they are ascending. There is a lot of anguish in those that haven't accepted the release from their physical bodies. Anguish and pain."

Machaneka was processing what Prentice had just said when their whirlwind seemed to come to a halt. At first, Phillip and Prentice stood at attention, seemingly alarmed. Then Phillip smiled and said, "A momentary setback in our travel. It seems that someone special is ascending. We get to see what I believe humans call a V.I.P. make their journey." Machaneka was delighted. What does that mean? What does it look like? And who is this person that is so important? As the three of them stood together looking out into the realm, she noticed that the entire realm had come to a halt. Every spirit in the spheres and on the rays of light had stopped their ascent.

As she watched in astonishment the sound of wings flapping in flight penetrated the whirlwind they were encased in and then she almost squealed. What appeared to be an army of angels, each with multiple sets of wings, soared from beneath them and took place on two sides of a blinding ray of light. As they assumed their positions, they each raised their wings to full attention. Coming through next was beyond incredible to see. The Seraphim angels, highest ranking known to man, were approaching with the fire of their power surrounding them. Machaneka swooned when she saw who they were escorting to heaven. The beloved Kelly who had assisted Odara in her last assignment was in the midst of the powerful angels. Kelly, the mother of the beautiful, gifted Apollo. The amazing soft-spoken champion for breast cancer who had been entrusted with the ability to access the women who rest in the hills and the book of names of the 64,000 missing African American women in the United States of America.

Machaneka's spirt was saddened for a moment. She knew that Apollo was still a baby and that Kelly's husband loved her immensely. The world had taken a big hit with the loss of her battle against breast cancer. That sadness was replaced quickly when Kelly's ascent reached nearer to the whirlwind. The beautiful dark cocoa-coated Kelly was radiating in the light. She was cloaked in a magnificently beaded gold gown and elaborate headdress that would have made an Egyptian goddess envious. Kelly was heavily jeweled, and her eyes were afire. She moved slowly and gracefully with the Seraphim as her guides to the heavens. Machaneka was proud. She knew that Kelly was going to do her best work from the spirit realm, and she knew that Apollo would have the greatest guardian angel of all time.

Phillip and Prentice did not take their eyes off her as she watched intently while Kelly made her ascent towards the heavens. Machaneka blinked back a couple of tears as Kelly ascended out of sight, and the sentry of angels who had flanked the light that she traveled on lowered their wings and dispersed. Prentice asked her if she was okay. She responded with a nod of her head and then realized that the whirlwind was in motion again. She had a question for Phillip, but she was afraid she knew the answer would be no. Phillip spoke before she could ask. "You have a request?"

Without hesitation she blurted out her questions. "Is there any possibility that I can go check on Apollo and Kelly's husband? I'm concerned about Older Odara as well. I keep getting flashes of her, but I can't seem to connect fully. I'm certain the Sacred Council would understand. We could release Odara's body, and I can go make sure that they are alright and then pick up here where we left off, couldn't we?" Phillip and Prentice had looks of bewilderment on their faces. As they were about to respond to her question the whirlwind dissipated and the three of them were standing near a small lake that was bordered by calla lilies. There were lotus flowers floating on the lake and butterflies of all colors and sizes fluttering everywhere. The sky was hazy with a light, misty fog and the fragrant smell of fresh lavender permeated the air.

Machaneka smiled when she saw glittering sparkles of light begin to appear amongst the calla lilies. She knew exactly where she was. As a young spirit warrior, she had been assigned to the mystical realm where fairies prevailed and thrived. She was inexperienced and was not successful in fully defeating the enemy that was trying to turn the realm of love and magic into a dark and evil place. She had almost forgotten her question when Phillip addressed her sternly.

"The insult of requesting to abort the assignment given to you by the Sacred Council in an effort to prepare you for the highest promotion that can be afforded a spirit warrior is beyond my comprehension, which by the way is quite extensive. You continue to amaze me with your attachment to humans and their trials. However, because I am so fond of you and respect your odd affinity for them and the compassion that almost always gets you into unnecessary predicaments, I will make one allowance for you to have a VISUAL of them. You have a few moments to tune in and see them. Then we must continue ahead. The second moon is rising tonight, and you are expected to be in the presence of two powerful ancients, the beautiful, magical McKenzie and Lizzie of this mystical realm. Please be quick about it."

Machaneka hesitated. She was partially ashamed that she was being chastised by Phillip for her inconsideration and lack of gratitude. She was also torn because of the deep emotion that moved her to make her request in the first place. She turned to Prentice in hopes of some sort of support. Prentice simply shook his head and said, "What will it take for you to understand who and what you are?"

Machaneka dropped her head and then turned to Phillip. "I will check on all of them when I have reassumed the body of Odara. I am ready to move on with our journey." Phillip and Prentice exhaled and the three of them stood on the bank of the lake appreciating its beauty and magnificence.

3

The Second Moon

McKenzie and Lizzie stood side by side facing the Pond of Wishes. The morning sunrays bounced off the ripples of water and sporadically produced rainbows that graced the banks of the pond. This was their favorite place in the realm that they resided in, and it continued, after centuries, to be as beautiful as it was when they were both young fairies. They were expecting a visit from their old friend Machaneka. They had both been given explicit detail about what could and could not happen during this visit. On the wings of a dove, a message had been sent to them from the Sacred Council. Their beloved Machaneka was in position to receive a grand promotion, and throughout the course of five moons she would revisit places where her development as a spirit warrior had been critical.

The exception that was granted to McKenzie and Lizzie was that they would be the sole part of that journey where Machaneka would be allowed to speak with them and interact. The rest of her journeys were for viewing and acknowledgement only.

Lizzie was excited and losing patience while awaiting the arrival of their old friend. McKenzie, feeling the unrest of her lifelong companion, smiled at her and said, "It won't be long, I heard the drums of sacred travel earlier."

Lizzie smiled back at her and regained her regal composure. "I just want to see how she has grown; she was in the first season of her creation when she came to assist us." They both took a deep breath and stared across the pond into the distant forest looking for a sign of arrival. It seemed like hours went by, but it was only moments later when a Sentry Fairy, cloaked in lavender appeared beside them.

"Your Highnesses! You have guests requesting entry into the veiled realm, shall I admit them or send them away?"

Mckenzie turned to the sergeant of her protective guards and asked, "Is one of them a spirit warrior named Machaneka?"

The sergeant lowered his wings and raised his hand to his head in full salute. "Yes, your highness, and she is traveling with Phillip, the messenger for the Sacred Council as well as Prentice!"

Mckenzie and Lizzie's wings fluttered, and the wind swirled around them with prisms of glittery light. Not only was their friend here, but she was being escorted by Phillip AND Prentice!

Now they understood how important this journey was for her, and most importantly, they understood that the young soldier that they knew was no more. To be escorted by Phillip was almost a standard under these circumstances, but to be accompanied by Prentice meant that there was an absolute magnitude of power involved that Machaneka may not even know of yet. "Open the veil for our guests immediately, please, and thank you for not delaying the knowledge of their request." Mckenzie lowered her wings and nodded approval toward the sergeant, and in the blink of an eye he was gone.

Machaneka, Phillip, and Prentice were standing on the bank of a beautiful lake in silence. Machaneka tried to remember the lake form her previous visit there, but it wasn't coming to her at all. Phillip spoke as if he was reading her mind. "None of what you see at the moment will be what you remember. When the realm was camouflaged by the Sacred Council to protect it, so were the entry points to the queens' kingdoms. They should know by now that we have arrived. You will see familiar territory when the veil is lifted to allow for us to enter." Machaneka closed her eyes in anticipation. Mckenzie and Lizzie were majestic fairy queens, and they were her first experience with magic and fantasy.

She remembered being overwhelmed by everything about their presence and fascinated when she found out that they were older than the Sacred Council that she served.

While deep in thought she heard chimes and small bells fill the air. She opened her eyes just as Prentice was saying, "I love this part." The lake that they stood on the bank of began to swirl and the waters began to recede. Then a fountain of water sprang forth from the center as birds, butterflies, and welcome fairies flew from the spewing fountain.

The grass around the bank of the lake turned to a lush green while orchids, roses, chrysanthemums, and lilies sprouted everywhere.

The fluttering wings of the welcome fairies produced glittery sparkles everywhere, and as the fountain filled the reservoir to capacity, Machaneka began to see what she remembered as a magical paradise. When the fountain stopped its flow, standing on the bank of the Pond of Wishes next to them was McKenzie and Lizzie. Machaneka, even in the power that she had acquired as a matured spirit warrior for the Sacred Council, was speechless and almost swooned at their presence. Prentice reached for her hand. "Incredible, aren't they?" Machaneka could only nod her head in agreement. Phillip saw the wonder in Machaneka's eyes and then noticed that McKenzie and Lizzie were in the same state of astonishment. As McKenzie's eyes began to tear, Machaneka realized that they could see her! She turned to Phillip, and he answered before she could ask any questions. "The Sacred Council determined that the visit involving this part of your journey would prove most beneficial if communication was allowed because they were a critical part of your development in the beginning of your existence as a spirit warrior. You are free to speak and interact with them while we are here." Machaneka began to elevate without trying. As she rose above them the sunlight illuminated her as she spun around in joy.

Mckenzie and Lizzie watched in amazement while Machaneka spiraled in the air and the sun's illumination made her dark brown skin glow like it was on fire. When the tears that had begun to well in McKenzie's eyes began to fall, Prentice produced a crystal box from his robe, opened it, and placed it under Mckenzie's chin. She gracefully took the box and allowed her tears to fall into it. She then closed and passed the box to Lizzie who also captured her tears in the box.

As Machaneka returned to the ground they closed the box and handed it back to Prentice. Prentice lowered to one knee and accepted the box and immediately placed in the folds of his robe. Looking at Machaneka, he spoke quietly. "The tears of a fairy queen can save lives and nations. They should never hit the ground. These will be preserved by the Sacred Council and presented to a deserving spirit warrior for their Sacred Chest." Machaneka was listening but not really paying attention, as she and her old friends were locked in gazes with one another. Mckenzie and Lizzie stepped towards her in unison and took her by the hands while Phillip and Prentice watched in amazement as the atmosphere around them came alive.

When McKenzie and Lizzie took Machaneka by the hands she felt the fire that she was created from surge through her body. No one had spoken a word yet. Machaneka's foot and a half of natural curls sprang to life and began to blow in the wind. The orange and gold gown that she was wearing started sparkling and the flame in the middle of the amulet on her forehead began to glow like it had been lit.

Mckenzie, the tallest of the two fairy queens had released herself from her emerald-studded robing and several sets of translucent wings began to softly flutter, each movement from them releasing flower petals and starbursts while her waist length braids began to arrange themselves into a bun atop of her head graced with white roses. Lizzie smiled as she looked into the eyes of Machaneka, her wings expanded and spread to full width colored with golden and lilac swirls that danced across them.

While they took the time to accept each other's presence, the sky began to turn a radiant lavender, pink, and purple. The flowers that had begun to bloom when the veil was lifted for the entry of their guests, started multiplying, and the nearby trees extended their branches up and outward towards the sky while their leaves sprouted and covered them, creating an archway that extended for miles. It was that point that Machaneka heard the singing. The wind fairies were swirling above them, their wings in motion creating a melody that sounded like a choir singing in unison.

Phillip was mesmerized. He had heard tales of the heavily shrouded and protected realm of the fairies where beauty, wonder, and magic were always present. He had dismissed most of what he had heard to be spiritual folklore, but actually witnessing what was happening just at the touch of the two fairy queens with Machaneka had absolutely convinced him that what he had heard was truth.

Prentice chuckled as a young wisdom fairy flittered back and forth between his shoulder spans.

Obviously intrigued by his size and his observance of her without any response, the fairy flew from his head to his feet and then back again. She flew up to his face and stared into his eyes, then to his ears and his nose studying him before landing and resting on one of his folded arms. She stared at him with her eyes gleaming and turned her head from side to side. He knew that she was trying to figure out not who but what he was. Sitting on his forearm she was so incredibly tiny compared to him. Never taking her eyes from his, she cradled in the fold between his forearm and his biceps having exhausted herself exploring his body. Then she took a deep breath and relaxed. Machaneka and the fairy queens laughed aloud as Prentice maintained his composure so that she could rest. "You have an admirer, Prentice. As usual you have captured the attention of one of us." McKenzie blew the wisdom fairy a kiss and she was rejuvenated. She slowly flew back up to look Prentice in the eye one last time and then she flew away. Prentice remained motionless, aware that Machaneka's curiosity could be a distraction if it was peaked.

Machaneka heard McKenzie clearly. Prentice was not a stranger to the fairy queen. Lizzie interrupted her thought process. "Prentice has been here on many occasions before the veil. He has been a great friend and protector. We go back to a time before the Sacred Council was created." Machaneka hung on her every word.

Now she had even more questions about her companion. Who is he really? What does he do for the Sacred Council, and what power does he possess that she has no idea about? The questions were flooding her mind until McKenzie spoke. "It is an honor to be in your presence and witness the growth that you have acquired. You are no longer the rambunctious, fiery but unsure young warrior that came to assist us during a time of war. You, Machaneka, are a gift to behold, absolutely beautiful, magnificent, and you have personified your power." Machaneka looked at the face of the ancient fairy queen whose appearance was still youthful. She was humbled by her words.

Lizzie took advantage of Machaneka's silence and spoke next. "We speak often of you and your bravery, the fierceness that you exhibited even when you were afraid and unsure. Your desire to help keep us safe will never go unmentioned or unappreciated." Machaneka tried to remember everything that happened several centuries ago. There had been so many other assignments since then, hundreds of them, some large and dangerous, some small. She struggled recalling all of her time with the fairy queens.

Even though the love she felt was as strong as it was when she last saw them, the assignment was only coming to her in a blur of memories. Lizzie saw that Machaneka appeared to be unsure of all that had occurred. She released Machaneka's hand and turned to Phillip and Prentice. "Behold and bear witness to why we are still in existence in this realm." Then she turned back to Machaneka and cupped her face in both of her hands. "Remember, warrior, remember so that you can see that you have always been who you are now." Lizzie kissed Machaneka on the forehead and a sphere of light arose above her head. Machaneka looked up into the sphere and then closed her eyes. It all came flooding back to her in vivid memory.

'The Sacred Council was in a frenzy. One of the oldest realms in the universe was under attack and it was the result of carelessness and underestimation. Isis had spoken to the reigning Queen Fairy about fairies of any kind visiting other realms, especially the earth realm where power was so desperately craved by human beings. She had also tried to warn the queen that a juvenile fairy could be captured and influenced by evil energies and that would put their realm at risk. The Queen Fairy McKenzie assured Isis that she had made a mandate that there would always be no travel outside of their realm except under extreme circumstances and with a senior fairy escort. Unfortunately, McKenzie wasn't aware that a young curious pixie had already left for the Earth realm and had been trying to assimilate in a small mountain town in North Carolina for some time. Unbeknownst to that pixie, the town that she had chosen was a wiccan community, and one of the strongest sorceresses on the planet lived in that town with an entire coven of witches that practiced black magic. The pixie, thinking that she could blend in and pass as a youth while learning the ways of humans, crossed paths with the evil sorceress Onique Exal almost immediately upon her arrival.

Onique recognized instantly that something was different about the young pixie and was determined to find out who she was and why she was there.

Onique pretended to befriend the young pixie and quickly charmed her into believing that she cared deeply for her wellbeing. After some time, the pixie began to feel safe and comforted while in the presence of Onique. It was at this point that the young pixie in her naivety made a grave mistake. She revealed that she was a fairy from the ancient realm of Magia. The sorceress wasted no time in acting. With the intent of taking over another realm that was full of powerful magic where she could rule with her coven for evil, she began to slowly poison the pixie every time she visited her. The pixie was completely unaware that she was being fed concoctions that would weaken her loyalty to the great fairy queens McKenzie and Lizzie and would also create a desire to be powerful and respected.

Eventually, she began to weaken in her strength as a fairy and doubt that the love and respect that she had received at home in her own realm was genuine. The sorceress who had waited patiently for her potions to take effect, saw that the pixie was beginning to exhibit human-like emotions and reactions to things more and more on a daily basis.

She convinced the young pixie that she deserved to be as powerful as the queens that she served. She began brainwashing the pixie into believing that if she were to take her and her "friends" back to the realm with her, that they would help her to convince the fairy queens to promote her to a position of royalty where she would be appropriately respected and have servants that would worship her. The pixie began to believe the sorceress and trust her completely.

Onique had gathered her coven together and began to prepare them for the events that were to come next. They met every day to plan how they would infiltrate the realm of Magia and take over with black magic, becoming all powerful and commandeering the elements of evil in a land of their own. Onique had the young pixie come to a coven meeting where she introduced her to who she described as her friends. Then told her to show them how to open the portal to her realm so that they could go there with her and campaign on her behalf. The pixie, who had never fully shown herself to anyone in the town, stepped out of her dress and cloak, and the coven was astounded. Her emerald green and golden wings opened up behind her and she flew above them. Glittery rays of light beamed from her wings as she looked around the room. The pixie took out a wand and began drawing a stream of images in the air with it. She completed the portal entry by encircling the room and blowing a small puff of fairy dust into the air. Onique and the coven were motionless, poised for attack as a doorway appeared in front of them. When the door opened the pixie motioned for them to follow her. Not knowing what was about to happen, when they entered the realm, the pixie excitedly turned to her companions to show them which way to go to speak to the fairy queens. It only took a moment after the portal closed for her to realize that she had been deceived.

When the last of the coven had passed through the portal, Onique and two hundred witches stood alongside the Pond of Wishes. They immediately began to reveal themselves as they howled and snarled, their dark powers feeling as if they had been enhanced by being in a land of magic. The flowers, grass, and trees within proximity began to wilt and wither as the evil they had brought with them filled the air.

The pixie was mortified by the sight of seeing them transform before her eyes from smiling, peasant women into glowering evil. Onique tried to grab the pixie, but she wasn't quick enough. Being back in her own realm had given full restoral to her fairy powers and she flew away from Onique at the speed of light, making herself invisible as she shot towards the fairy queens' castle to warn them of what she had done.

The chaos that ensued within the next few minutes changed the trajectory of the realm of Magia forever. The Sacred Council and the fairy queens were simultaneously alerted to an intrusion with the instantaneous rotting of the living plants, trees, and flowers. Because everything in the realm of Magia was alive as a breathing individual would be, when they started to die, it caused a ripple in the waves of the universe. The Holy Trinity of the Sacred Council was absolute in sending the newly created spirit warrior Machaneka to assist in the fight against evil. Shango and Oya believed a more experienced warrior should go.

Isis asked the Holy Trinity, why Machaneka, and the response was that Machaneka was created from fire and infused with love, a depth of love that surpassed most other warriors, and the only thing that can disperse darkness – was light. Isis understood him immediately and sent Phillip to send Machaneka on her way.

While Machaneka was being summoned to that part of the universe, the fairy queens McKenzie and Lizzie had already assembled thousands of war fairies to protect their home. The coven of witches had begun to shapeshift into giant eagles with massive talons, poisonous serpents, and wolves with enormous drooling fangs. They were attacking and trying to kill everything that they could as the evil sorceress Onique assumed the body of a giant fire breathing Komodo dragon. She stretched out to be almost twelve feet and over four hundred pounds. In a frenzy from the desire to destroy everything in her path, she was heading to the fairy queen castle, setting everything in her path afire.

Some of the warrior fairies took the air to battle with the eagles while others tried to gain ground with the serpents and wolves. Onique had prepared her coven for the battle well; they consistently changed shapes and cast spells that brought many fairies to their demise on the ground. The eagles were gaining ground as well, by snatching the fairies up and trying to shred them. Onique had one plan, to get to the palace of the fairy queens and take control of the Book of Magic. She knew if she got ahold of it, that she could cast a spell that would make all the fairies be forever bound to her. What she was not prepared for was the power of the fairy queens combined, and she had no knowledge of spirit warriors.

McKenzie and Lizzie cast a protection spell over their palace that made it camouflage into the surrounding trees and foliage. They then stood face to face to strengthen themselves. In understanding that they were up against something quite strong, they wanted to be sure that they had no weaknesses between them. They held hands and transferred to one another whatever the other queen had less of. The sky began to rumble and swirl, and the ground shook as they opened themselves up for the transfers of power. The wings of both queens expanded and increased in size as a golden light filled the room, and their eyes and hair glimmered as if laced with diamond dust. They released one another and issued a command.

"Delspeth Plividus!" Startled, Onique came to a halt as she found herself face to face with the two fairy queens. Upon sight, Mckenzie knew that

Onique was a sorceress with great power. She pulled a sliver of light from one of her wings and struck Onique with it, blinding her upon contact.

Making no haste Lizzie began to bind Onique with a holding spell. Onique was only stunned for a brief moment. She regained her sight, and in a rage, before she could be completely bound, she spewed a raging flame at Lizzie. To her surprise the flames met another person who completely blocked them from touching Lizzie. Onique reared her head to see what had protected the fairy queen. Standing in front of Lizzie was Machaneka, the young spirit warrior sent by the Sacred Council to assist the fairy queens in protecting their realm.

Machaneka was created from fire and could not be harmed by it. The flames from the mouth of the Komodo dragon hit Machaneka's body and became a part of her. She then summoned the light of the sun from Ametratsu, the Japanese Sun Goddess of the Sacred Council. Using the sacred language of spirit warriors she yelled towards the sky. "Ametratsu! Wohiballaka! Asmeshinakat! Solibantunek Now!"

The fairy queens braced themselves together with Machaneka who had outstretched her arms to them as the sky in the Magia realm was filled with rays of sunlight that was blinding. Onique was not a match for a summon from the Sun Goddess who represented fertility and who made plants grow that gave life to humans and Gods alike. The sorceress tried to swing her massive, powerful tail at the trio standing together near her but the ground around her that had withered as she slithered her way to towards the palace came to life in great magnitude. Massive tree limbs sprang forth from the Earth and bound Onique to the ground as they wrapped around her body completely, securing her tail and her mouth so that she could not spit fire nor cast a spell.

Machaneka stepped away from the fairy queens as the sorceress tried to wrestle her way free, but she was wrapped like a mummy in tree limbs. She hissed and tried to howl but her monstrous jowls were not strong enough to break the binds. The grass around the sorceress had also been rejuvenated, and it began to weave a tight knit encasement over the tree limbs until it was completely covered. The fairy queens watched as Machaneka produced an orb of fire that she opened to seal the sorceress into.

"Bahillano, Mispathonus! The orb enclosed the sorceress into it, and Machaneka was about to send it to the realm of banishment when she heard the voice of the mighty Isis of the Sacred Council. "This evil must be destroyed completely; she will not have the mercy of the council to be able to live even in the desolate nothingness of the banishment realm. She has empowered too many that are doing more damage as I speak to the realm of Magia. When she is destroyed the others will lose all power and the remaining warrior fairies will be able to capture and destroy them all as well. Leave nothing of her, and her head must come off first."

Machaneka moved without hesitation. She told McKenzie and Lizzie to produce a barrier around her and the bound sorceress.

As they flew in a circle around her creating a wall of glistening light, Machaneka lifted her head towards the sky. The Thunder God Shango sent a lightning bolt to her which she caught with both hands. She understood that the first blow must be to sever the head of the evil Onique.

Because Onique had assumed the form of the Komodo dragon, she could not miscalculate the size of the beast that she couldn't see because of the tree limbs and the living grass encasement. She closed her eyes, unsure of what end the beast's head lay. In the stillness and silence of the moment the tightly bound Onique tried to hiss at her. Following the sound of the hissing, she raised the lightning bolt and brought it down in one strong swing. The encasement cracked open, and the tree limbs split apart as the head of the Kimodo dragon fell away from the body of the beast. Mckenzie and Lizzie, from outside of the barrier, and Machaneka, standing over her, watched as the dragon's head howled and turned into the head of Onique the evil sorceress. She was still trying to scream a spell but had no vocal cords. Machaneka wielded the lightning bolt like a sword again and cut the beast's body into several pieces. Once the tail had been cut in two, she dragged the lightning bolt around the perimeter of the body and drove the bolt into the head of the beast. The fairy queens watched in amazement as Machaneka opened both of her palms and balls of fire began to grow in them. She swirled them in the air several times until they joined together, and then she shot them into the perimeter that contained the beast.

As the evil Onique burned, screams and howls filled the air in the fairy kingdom. The coven had begun to lose all their powers and some of them began to die as Onique turned to ashes. Mckenzie and Lizzie lifted the protective barrier from around Machaneka and what once was Onique Exal. They were amazed and exhausted, but they had to make sure that the rest of the realm was safe before they could celebrate a victory. The next few days were spent surveying the damage that had been done. The pixie who had opened the portal to the realm was distraught with grief and shame. She was locked in a room in the queen's castle while they decided what her fate should be. The realm had been almost eviscerated. Troops of injured and destroyed fairies were everywhere. The fairy queens were heartbroken, but they knew that they would eventually be able to recover the realm and restore it. Machaneka received a message from the Sacred Council to stay there until every fairy and member of the coven had been accounted for. While she was there, the Sacred Council cloaked the realm of Magia so that it would be undiscoverable for outsiders forever.'

Machaneka opened her eyes and tears fell from them. McKenzie and Lizzie produced a flower crown and placed it on her head. Mckenzie spoke first. "We knew that you may not remember the intensity of the battle because we surrounded and cushioned you with deep love for the duration of your stay with us. We are forever indebted to you, Machaneka. You saved Lizzie's life and our realm from peril. We have honored you as a queen from the moment that you left us centuries ago."

Lizzie stepped forward and kissed her on the forehead. "You are one of us and more than us, forever, warrior. All you need to do is pluck a flower from this crown and we will be at your side instantaneously. We love you."

Machaneka was humbled by their gratitude and somewhat exhausted from the intensive recall of her time there. "I love you too, and I am only a water lily away from you at all times. I am ecstatic to see that you have restored your realm to the magnificence that it represents, and I am thrilled to see that your fairies have begun to replenish in numbers. I am thankful for you, old friends."

Neither Phillip nor Prentice had the words to convey what they felt from seeing Machaneka's recollection play out before them like a movie in living color. Prentice stood studying her. He was now aware that she really had no idea how much power she had been entrusted with – or did she? Phillip gathered himself together and spoke. "Thank you, Your Highnesses, for allowing us to enter your home. I am sorry to say that we must make haste. We need to be back on the other side of this realm because the third moon is approaching soon, and Machaneka has a decision to make with the close of the fifth moon. It's been too long since we've seen one another but I'm afraid that this visit must cease now." Mckenzie and Lizzie wrapped around Machaneka in a deep embrace and then stepped back.

As Phillip, Prentice, and Machaneka were encircled in a swirl of wind, Prentice produced the box of fairy queen tears. "I hope we never need them, but in case someone does, the Sacred Council thanks you." Mckenzie and Lizzie stood smiling, hands locked with one another as their visitors were swooped away.

4
Older Odara's Plight

Back at the chateau, Mutora and Roma were moving through the home in silence. They were tending to the basic maintenance and cleaning of the multiple rooms while simultaneously thinking about Machaneka and the decision that she needed to make. They had been together for multiple lifetimes, blessed with the opportunity to serve the Sacred Council by initiating spirit warriors into their physical vessels. They had often spoken about the way they felt when they brought Machaneka to life with her gifts. Asir, who had been present and assisted with her ceremony, was extremely excited about Machaneka from the moment they were assigned to her. He said more than once to them in conversation, "This one is not like the others." As they parted ways and Mutora and Roma were sent in a different direction from him, Mutora remembered that he stated Machaneka was one of his greatest assignments.

Looking back at the many others that they all had a hand in assisting to join the world in a human form, she noted that at the time, she had no idea why he felt that this particular spirit warrior was any more special or different from the others. From the time of Machaneka's conception and introduction to her physical body to now, Mutora and Roma had helped with hundreds of others in the same capacity. She did understand now though, why Asir was so adamant and proud. Machaneka was different from the others. She was as much human as she was spirit. Although she was only utilizing the bodies she was assigned to for a higher purpose, she used what was the best of their humanity in the same way that she used her gifts and powers as a spirit warrior. To the chagrin of the Sacred Council, Machaneka also allowed herself to feel.

Feelings were never supposed to be a part of the decision-making process of any spirit warrior, but Machaneka had managed to use the human side of her and incorporate her feelings into her decisions. For the most part, this could have been a catastrophe for her in many cases but usually ended up being her saving grace.

Mutora was proud of her. Machaneka had managed to survive several hundreds of years in several different bodies and constantly grow within her spirit while being conscious of her humanity. This last time around was different though. Machaneka had come to an impasse as a spiritual warrior for the Sacred Council. Because of her ability to feel so deeply, she had begun to question what it would be like to just have a full human experience. What it would feel like to work a job, have a family, build a home, and get a formal education. She was certain that the Sacred Council had retired her for her uncertainty since she hadn't been called for any assignments through two lifetimes. But she was wrong in that assumption. As soon as she had relaxed and was beginning to experience what she thought she wanted to experience, she was called back to assignments in the body of Odara.

Machaneka loved existing as Odara. She felt beautiful, empowered, free, and strong. Maybe that was why the Sacred Council began to assign her again. Possibly, she had gotten too comfortable, and they wanted her to remember who she was.

Mutora found herself standing at the door to the master bedroom where Odara lay in a state of rest, protected and surrounded by guardian angels. She wasn't sure what had drawn her there but looked up to see that Roma had joined her. They stood together in front of the doorway, unsure of what they were feeling. What they were sure of, was that something did not feel right.

What Mutora and Roma were sensing was not far from the truth at all. On the other side of the bedroom door, the guardian angels who were holding a protective vigil over Odara's resting body had all been brought to attention. She had been in a completely motionless state for a little over two months and suddenly her body was beginning to show signs of agitation. Samuel, the eldest and strongest of the angels over Odara's watch could not for any reason leave his post guarding the door to the bedroom. His charge was to protect the room and everything in it at all costs from his position. He noticed first that Odara's breathing pattern had changed and he motioned for the other angels in the room to take a precautionary position. Her breathing soon began to regulate and they all relaxed momentarily. Their relief was disrupted when Samuel saw Odara reach out into the air, then she grasped her womb and winced in silence with what looked like pain.

Immediately, the other angels who were at their posts in all four corners of the room flanked her body. Sincere and Sherrise, the delicate but mighty angels who were stationed in the two furthest corners from the door, joined hands above Odara's womb, and the light that emanated from their grasp of one another began to envelop Odara's lowerbody. Valerie and Benjamin who were stationed in the two closest corners of the room to the door beganprayer in unison, calling for peace and stability.Their voices were mighty and strong, causing the light fixtures in the room to sway. On the other sideof the sealed door, Mutora and Roma heard theprayers of the powerful angels fill the chateau, and they immediately assumed an attitude of prayer on their knees with their faces to the floor. As Odara's body began to relax and all signs of distress or pain dissipated, the angels inside of the room maintained their positions and their prayers. Once she had returned fully to her state of unrest, Samuel motioned for the other angels to return to their stations.

Samuel was concerned. Odara had been put into a state of rest because the spirit that inhabits her body was on a journey ordered by the Sacred Council. This meant that she pretty much was in a spiritually-induced coma, incapable of doing or feeling anything. She was disconnected completely until Machaneka reassumed her body. How then, did she go into some sort of state of arrest? He couldn't leave his post, but he would send a message to the Sacred Council that something was awry. Even though he had a powerful team of guardian angels in the room with him who could combat almost anything, he wanted to get a message to them about what he had just witnessed.

With the other angels back in their prospective corners, Samuel hadn't taken his eyes off Odara. She was magnificent even in her resting state. She radiated power even without Machaneka inside of her. He was honored to have been called to protect her. He raised his right hand towards her body and his left hand towards the light streams that surrounded her body for protection. He slowly pulled his left hand back towards his body and a stream of light followed his hand. Samuel used his right hand to follow the stream until it met his left hand. He then spoke to the light. "Show the Council." The light flickered and then changed shape. It presented itself in front of him like a small movie screen, the events of what had just happened playing over and over. Samuel rolled the light up like a scroll and then slid it under the bedroom door.

Mutora and Roma had just returned to their feet from the attitude of prayer and were about to express their concern for whatever had happened behind the bedroom door when a ray of light slid from under the bedroom door and rolled to their feet. Instinctively they knew that a message was being sent to the Sacred Council. Mutora retrieved the scroll of light and Roma followed her down the hall and stairs towards the great room. Neither of them had entered that room since the Sacred Council had visited and given Odara her options for promotion. When they entered the room and closed the heavy ornate doors, the room was still charged with energy that made everything in it feel alive. The plants were thriving despite having not been tended to in months. The floors were sparkling and the windows glistened. Mutora walked to the large window that always provided the most spectacular view of either the sun or the moon. Roma joined her by her side and placed both of her hands spread apart on the window. As Mutora held the scroll up to the window in the glowing moonlight, Roma spoke to the window.

"Be the door and the path, this message is to be in the presence of the Sacred Council NOW." They didn't move nor speak as the window began to quiver then vaporize. Mutora unwrapped a gold cord from one of her braids and placed it in the hand holding the scroll of light in the air. Then she released the scroll. They stood together and watched as the scroll now wrapped in the gold cord from her hair, took to the night air and then vanished. The Sacred Council would receive it, recognize the cord as hers and know that it is a message from them, and they would send some sort of acknowledgement. She and Roma would be firmly rooted where they stood until the acknowledgement came through.

After what felt like hours because of their anxiety about what that message was, a blue jay flew by and landed on the windowsill. In his beak was the gold cord that Mutora had wrapped the light scroll in. Mutora retrieved the cord and the blue jay gave her a polite curtsy and was gone. The window quivered again and solidified. Mutora and Roma, still unsure of anything but aware that something was not right, sat side by side on the beautiful, purple tufted velvet sofa that Odara loved and began to mentally prepare themselves for possible warfare.

Enveloped in a swirl of wind and cumulous clouds, Phillip, Prentice, and Machaneka had begun their journey back through the ascension realm to head towards the next dimension where Machaneka would visit four elders who were a very special part of her life as a spirit warrior. After they passed through the ascension realm, they would be on a direct path back to the planet Earth to Mount Huayna Picchu, the mountain that sits above Macchu Picchu in the Andes mountains of Peru. Mount Huayna Picchu was one of the most spectacular urban creations of the Inca empire and quite worthy of the presence of the four female elders who lived there. Phillip was particularly fond of the foursome.

Together they were an embodiment of love, and it was always pleasurable to be in their presence. He was about to ask Prentice if he was familiar with them when the wind that was transporting themcame to a halt. He and Prentice flanked Machaneka's sides and waited for the clouds to clearso that they could see what the disruption was.Machaneka was still in a state of euphoria from visiting McKenzie and Lizzie and had been quietly contemplating all that been brought to total recall for her. Phillip and Prentice flanking her sides snappedher out of her reverie.

"Is something wrong?" she asked. Before either of her companions could acknowledge her with an answer, the clouds rescinded from blocking their view. All of them were taken aback to see the entire Sacred Council gathered before them. Seeing no other activity around them, Machaneka was alarmed. She felt a sense of dread begin to fill her. Isis outstretched her hand, and a single eagle feather was in her palm. She held the feather up and then blew it towards the three of them. Prentice caught the feather and ran his hand over it. He then passed it to Phillip who did the same thing. Phillip dropped his head to not have to look at Machaneka as the Holy Trinity, Kali, and Amateratsu stepped forward to address them. The Holy Trinity in its divine glory spoke first.

"As unforeseen circumstances have arrived and even to us were unexpected, we have decided to provide you with some things that will help you to maintain your timeline of five moons and keep you from being severely distracted. My gift to you for this part of your journey is grace and discernment. Use it wisely and appropriately."

Kali smiled at Machaneka and spoke next. "I grant you a time exception that may be used once and once only. You will know when to use it to stop time long enough for you to do what you need do."

Amateratsu looked past Machaneka at Phillip and Prentice. "She will need your support at a time when you will not be certain of how to assist her. I give you both the residue from a sunbeam. When she cries out and you feel helpless, and you will, anoint her face and palms with the residue." When Amateratsu finished speaking, the Council crossed their hands over their hearts and was gone. The wind that was their transport did not immediately resume their journey.

Machaneka looked at Phillip and Prentice puzzled. "What is going on? What is happening that is so serious that the Sacred Council would meet us during our journey through the ascension realm with gifts to assist me? They each gave me what they thought I needed before we left the chateau. SAY SOMETHING PLEASE!"

Prentice took her by the hands and spoke softly. "The elder Odara is extremely ill. She is fighting for her life and not winning the fight. Because of that, your beloved Odara is also struggling to be at peace. Since they are the same person in two bodies, your Odara will feel the elder Odara's pain and will have to endure everything that the elder endures. The problem is that because you are the spirit that fuels her, and you are absent from her body, she will have to fight for life without your support to survive what elder Odara is dealing with." Machaneka was shaken. She looked at Phillip hoping that he would say something that would ease her or give her a glimpse of what to do. Unfortunately, the messenger was silent. His eyes were full of empathy, but he had no words that could help alleviate what she was feeling.

With tears in her eyes, she asked, "Are you telling me that Odara could die along with the elder Odara while I am on this assignment? This cannot be! There must be something that can be done. I am a spirit warrior for the second sentry of the Sacred Council of the Universe! My job is to SAVE lives! What do I do?" In her agitation Machaneka had begun to levitate, her hair had sprung to life, and the fire that she was created from had begun to spark in her palms. Prentice felt for her, he knew what she must do but he also knew that he could not tell her. This part of her journey had to be decided and traveled based solely on her own decisions. Machaneka then addressed him. "If you cannot tell me what to do, at least tell me what can be done!"

Prentice looked at Phillip who nodded his head slowly. "The Sacred Council has provided you with extra gifts to get you through this dilemma," Prentice said. "I can only say to you that the only way for the elder to survive is for you to give her breath from your spirit. If you do that…"

Before he could finish his sentence, Machaneka said, "Take me to her now!"

Phillip and Prentice responded in unison. "We cannot go there yet. You will be allowed to see her but not until the fourth moon." Machaneka was almost despondent as the information that she had been given and the inability to go to the elder Odara was processing in her mind. Then she lowered herself and stood still to get her bearings.

"Very well then, I call upon the gift from the great Kali, to suspend time as we find and visit the ultimate lightworker Trevelyn. I will need the crystals that she harvests and a divination spell from her when I go to see the elder during the fourth moon. She was last in Brazil, but I don't sense her there now. I will locate her, and you will accompany me to her location."

Machaneka closed her eyes and began to speak in the ancient tongue of the spirit warriors. "Lamiwehelata, shavilitus dolus mavinateus solobeha - Reveal yourself!" Phillip and Prentice watched as Machankea in her full poweroutstretched her palms and a small fire burst began to grow. As it grew from the size of a quarter to the size of a softball, sparks flew from it and formed a casing around it. Once the casing covered the entirefireball, Machaneka blew into it and it turned to ashes. Machaneka looked into the palms of her hands, and resting amongst the ashes were an emerald, a sapphire, and two rubies. She immediately knew exactly where her old friend and mentor Trevelyn was residing. She called out to the wind. "Take us to Sri Lanka, home of Trevelyn, keeper of all healing secrets through the magnificence of divinely harvested crystals!"

Phillip and Prentice spoke to the wind that was their transport in unison. "Take us there now!" The wind and clouds swirled around them until they were no longer visible, and at the speed of light, they were whisked through the ascension realm to the planet Earth headed for Sri Lanka – to see the great and mystical Trevelyn Drumer.

Machaneka was visibly upset, and her fear had inspired the determination to make sure that she would be able to help the elder Odara. As the wind settled and they all stood standing on the coast of Sri Lanka, Machaneka wasted no time and did not address her companions. She opened her right palm, and a fiery orb was released from it. Taking the precious gemstones that were still in her other hand, she placed them in the orb and said, "Show us the way." Prentice was in awe of the power she had in her command of fire. He watched silently with Phillip as the orb began to spin in Machaneka's hand, and then it rose into the air and began moving ahead of them. The orb was moving quickly and deliberately. They would not be able to keep up on foot, so they took flight behind it. Their journey was not a long one. About two miles up the coast the orb began to expand. As it got larger it moved more quickly until it stopped and hovered before them. Machaneka opened her hand and the orb returned to her palm which she closed and then reopened with the stones sitting in it.

Looking forward without the orb restricting their view, a small cottage sat a few hundred yards away, and sitting on the porch of the cottage in a rocking chair, sipping a cup of tea, was Trevelyn Drumer. The traveling trio returned to the ground and began walking up the pathway to the cottage. It was literally sitting in the middle of nothing else. The walkway was lined with beautifully colored stones and crystals. Some of them sparkled in the afternoon sun. Some of them were carefully wrapped in wire that was shaped like flowers, and some of them were almost three to five feet tall; magnificent in their markings and shape. As they grew closer, Trevelyn stood to greet them. Machaneka stopped before reaching the porch and bowed to her former mentor and old friend. Trevelyn returned the bow and then extended her arms. Machaneka almost ran to her and hugged her. Trevelyn held her for a moment and then stepped back to look at her. She was astounded at the strong, vibrant spirit warrior standing before her. It had been centuries since she had seen her, and Machaneka had become more magnificent than she ever could have imagined.

Machaneka stepped aside and introduced Phillip and Prentice to Trevelyn who both bowed to her and then expressed their honor to meet her. The men had both been silent until they were introduced. It was obvious that the connection between the two women was one of great respect and honor, so they waited to be included in their interaction. Phillip jokingly spoke to Trevelyn.

"Ms. Trevelyn, my apologies if the sight of a fiery orb hovering near your home alarmed you."

Trevelyn chuckled. "No worries here, I knew who was coming. The only time I get a visit that begins with the presence of fire, it is this amazing one right here. And please, call me Trev." Lovingly glancing towards Machaneka, Trevelyn turned and told her guests to join her in her home. As she escorted them in, Trevelyn addressed Prentice. "I have had the honor of learning about Phillip through Machaneka. I unfortunately am not familiar with you although quite aware that you are the elder amongst you all AND the power force. I have no secrets, nor questions, Prentice. You have questions and plenty that has not been revealed to your companions. I am not interested in what hasn't been shared by you. I would just like for you to relax because whatever brought Machaneka to me will require a spirit of peace in my space. I am not of the spirit realm but have been quite blessed by interacting with several who reside there. I'll allow you a moment to read me so that we can move ahead. Your energy is quite intense, and the uncertainty is unsettling. I can imagine you're wondering how you've never encountered me. The answer is simply that you've had no need to. So go ahead and check me out."

Prentice was caught off guard by Trevelyn's statements. Even more so that she was correct. He did not respond to her verbally. He stepped closer to her and placed a hand on her shoulder. Upon contact he changed his form to that of a hooded shawl that draped Trevelyn's upper body. Trevelyn was not fazed by the shifting of his shape. She wrapped the shawl closer to her body and smiled at Machaneka. Then she closed her eyes for a few minutes. Phillip and Machaneka patiently waited as Trev hummed a tune while holding the shawl close to her body. Just as quickly as it had begun, the shawl vanished and Prentice had reassumed his form. He and Trevelyn stood face to face and then Prentice took a knee and said, "It is an honor to know you."

Trevelyn covered her heart with her hands and responded, "The honor is all mine." The room was silent as Prentice maintained the position of respect, and Trevelyn held her heart, inhaling and exhaling deeply and slowly. A couple of tears rolled out the side of her eye and Machaneka was startled. Prentice rose to his feet and then Trevelyn invited them to have a seat.

Machaneka had questions but before she could ask any of them Trevelyn spoke to her. "Don't ask because it's none of your business, at least not yet. Just know that you are in the best of hands. The companion the Sacred Council provided you with is everything and more than you can digest right now.

Just have a seat so that we can take care of why you're here." Phillip chuckled. Prentice looked directly at Machaneka. She sent him a message telepathically. "Who are you?"

Prentice responded to her nonverbally as well. "I am who I am, and for now, I am here solely for you."

Trevelyn raised her hand. "There will be none of that, we speak aloud and in English around here."

"Thank you!" Phillip responded. Machaneka responded to Trevelyn's maternal tone by bowing her head and then sitting up straight. It was at that moment that she began to look around her surroundings. Seemingly, they all had begun to look around at about the same time. Trevelyn gave them a moment to digest the intensity and beauty of the room they were seated in. She understood her home was nothing like anything most people would ever imagine. Even those from the supernatural realm were going to be intrigued by the energy forces that she had carefully chosen for the décor in her home by the strategic placement of crystals and gemstones.

Machaneka, Phillip, and Prentice were seated on a large overstuffed white sofa that felt like sitting on a cloud. There were white, gold, and purple silk pillows on each end of the sofa. Each of them had already found a focal point of fascination. Machaneka had been to places where Trevelyn had lived before, but this place was most definitely the most exquisite of them all. Phillip had his eyes on the large sculpture of a single pair of magnificent wings by the front door. The sculpture carved from black obsidian almost seemed alive, as if the wings could take flight at any moment. While Phillip marveled at the detail and the beauty of the sculpture, Prentice was fixated on a set of three small amber bowls encrusted with diamonds that sat on the fireplace mantle. Machaneka had seen these pieces before, and while they were still beautiful to behold, her gaze was drawn to the curtain of rose quartz and amethyst that hung in the middle of the room from the ceiling. It was simple and still captivating. Rows and rows of the stones were strung together on individual silk cords with crystal quartz sporadically placed between them on the rows. At first glance the curtain looked like a floating array of stones, but the beauty of it was revealed when you notice after looking at it for a moment that the pattern of the stones created a large purple rose with pink tips on the petals. "That is one of my favorite pieces," Trevelyn said to Machaneka.

"The obsidian by the door, Phillip, was a gift from an Indian chief long ago who wanted to thank me for the crystals that I charged and blessed for his newborn daughter who came into this life with some physical challenges. Obsidian is a strongly protective stone that forms a shield against negativity. It is deliberately placed at my front door, wherever I reside. There have been visitors who got to my front door and were unable to move themselves further to enter my home."

Phillip was impressed. "It is quite a magnificent piece to say the least.

"The curtain that Machaneka is taken with is laced with rose quartz and amethyst. It is also deliberately placed in the center of this home. It purifies the air and enhances spiritual protection. The combination of amethyst and rose quartz together provides a substantial energy field that balances the other energies in the house. The amber bowls that have caught the attention of Prentice are encased with diamonds and were a gift from a priest at a monastery. They were given to me after a month of silence and meditation. Amber draws disease from the body, draws out negative energies from the aura, and transforms them into clear positive energy. The diamonds serve a similar purpose and vibrate at a high frequency."

"So now, let's get to the point of your visit. I'm certain that you have a purpose for being here. No one ever visits me for social reasons. That is not a bad thing by the way. I'm not usually too fond of or open to the energies of random people." Trevelyn laughed to herself for a moment. "Yeah, for real." Machaneka was tickled that Trevelyn hadn't changed and that she still got a kick out of herself. The same no nonsense, roll with the punches Trev that she remembered.

Machaneka began telling Trev about her existence in the body of Odara and how the elder Odara came into the picture. Then she shared with her the five-moon timeline that she had to make a decision about accepting full ascension or continuing to operate in the body of Odara for as long as she could. She shared with her the message from Isis about the elder Odara being ill and that she wanted to know if she had something that would assist her in saving the elder's life. When Machaneka stopped speaking she took a deep breath and looked at her old friend Trevelyn, her eyes pleading for a response that would give her a sense of hope. She innately knew that time was of the essence, and now that she was aware of the elder Odara's plight, she also knew that the old woman was slowly declining, headed towards death.

Trevelyn took a deep breath and closed her eyes. "Wow, that's a lot, babe. That's a whole lot to digest and even more to address. Since this woman is directly connected to you in such an intimate way, I need to process how and if I can help you. I understand that time is critical, but I need to take all of what you said in, work through it, pray on it, and then I can give you what I've come up with. I'm thankful that you were given a time reprieve to handle this because I need to sleep on this. You all may rest in any of the bedrooms that you feel comfortable in. There is also a detached bedroom in the backyard in my mineral garden that you will find peaceful and something to the tune of perfection for anyone desiring blissful rest. I will be unavailable for conversation until this time tomorrow when I will rejoin you all right here.

There's plenty of food, should you want to recharge the vessels you've chosen for this visit, and there's a library down the hall with books on any subject under the sun on the bookshelves. Help yourselves." Trevelyn stood and then nodded at Phillip and Prentice. Then she looked at Machaneka and said, "I'll do what I can with the best of what I have, but you need be prepared for the fact that no matter what you or I do, you cannot change someone's destiny or fate without paying a price." Trevelyn turned and headed down the hallway in her home. A door opened and closed, then another one. They heard cabinet doors opening and closing and drawers being pulled out. Then Trevelyn reappeared walking past them. She was wearing a heavily jeweled purple robe and carrying a small sachet, a vial, and a bucket covered in abalone shells. Her silver dreadlocks ornamented with cowrie shells had been pulled up into a bun on the top of her head and a small amethyst with a row of diamonds and sapphires hung in the middle of her forehead. Trevelyn glided past her visitors as if they were not there. She was humming and mumbling to herself. They were not of concern to her for the moment; she had already tuned in to the work she needed to do. Trevelyn walked out of the front door and down the walkway in the direction of the Indian Ocean that surrounded the coast that she lived on.

Phillip stood and announced that he was going to explore the rest of the home and figure out where he would rest. He also expressed curiosity about what someone like Trevelyn would have in her kitchen to prepare a proper meal with. "This is turning out to be a nice little detour. I've never been interested in humans with their little gifts of natural healing. I'm intrigued and must take the time to learn more. I shall begin with the mineral garden in the backyard and then make my way to the library to further educate myself. If I see something I can work with I will prepare us a meal. It's been quite some time since I was able to actually cook in a kitchen."

Prentice was watching Machaneka who hadn't moved or said a word since she told Trevelyn why they were there. She sensed his concern. "I'm fine, thank you," she assured him. "Just a bit anxious. I think I will walk around the home and property as well. Everything is so beautiful and mystical; it will provide a welcoming distraction until I go to sleep tonight."

Prentice nodded his head in acceptance of her statement. "I am interested in the detached bedroom in the mineral garden in the backyard," he said. My exploration of the incredible Trevelyn's world will begin there. They all stood and headed in different directions. Phillip started in the kitchen instead of heading outside while Prentice headed to the detached bedroom, and Machaneka went out the front door to marvel at the gardens that graced the perimeter of the cottage.

As Phillip, Prentice, and Machaneka were finding their way around her home, Trevelyn had reached the spot she had set out for to meditate, pray, and seek guidance from the ancestors in an effort to help Machaneka. She loosened the belt of her robe and it fell around her like a blanket. Nude, she anointed her body and temples, then sat Indian style on her robe and inhaled the fresh ocean air. She took the small sachet and opened it. Spreading the contents of the rarest of gold and jewels out in front of her as an offering, she closed her eyes and began her meditational process. She would remain in this position for as long as it took for her to reach the state of Samadhi. Samadhi was the highest level of meditation that happens spontaneously. Once in that state, Trevelyn would experience pure awareness and consciousness along with feeling like she has transcended the limitations of her body. It is the state that she needed to be in to find the answers that she was seeking to help her beloved Machaneka.

The day was quickly turning into the evening, and as the sun and moon began to exchange places, Machaneka had come back into the house and found the room where she would rest for the evening. The second bedroom in the cottage home was perfect for her. A large bed with turquoise and orange pillows atop a peacock patterned quilt sat directly beneath a window draped in orange silk curtains. Small statues of Oshun and elephant and peacock sculptures were atop the dresser, nightstands, and a small shelf.

There was an enormous dreamcatcher laced with stones representing the Chakras hanging in the middle of the wall directly across from the window. There was a fluffy turquoise rug that covered the majority of the floor, and there were two standing candelabras, one on each side of the bed. Machaneka smiled and exited the room, having claimed it as her space until the following afternoon.

She headed towards the kitchen where something was smelling divinely delicious. When she joined Phillip, he was a sight to see. He had put on an apron that he found in the kitchen. He was barefoot and his sleeves were rolled up. Never ever imagining seeing him in such a casual state, Machaneka laughed aloud.

As he stirred something carefully on the stovetop, he laughed aloud himself.

"Go ahead and enjoy this, Machaneka, as you will probably never get to experience it again. I'm sure you had no idea before that I could cook, but I'll have you know that before I became the messenger for the Sacred Council, long before your existence, I lived a full human experience and mastered a few culinary skills. We'll see if you laugh when you taste what I have prepared." Machaneka leaned up against the doorway to the kitchen. She had never thought of Phillip in any fashion other than that of the messenger. She wanted to ask him about the life that he once had but she noticed that he had gotten quiet, almost seemed to have withdrawn since he made his statement. She decided to leave it alone for now.

"I look forward to experiencing your culinary delight, Phillip, I cannot wait." Phillip smiled at her but still seemed distracted as he began chopping red onions. "I won't even bother to ask what you are preparing because it doesn't matter. If it tastes like it smells I will be in a very happy place when I go to bed." Once again Phillip did not respond. He continued with his prep work for whatever else he was preparing in silence. Something in his memory of his life before the Sacred Council had obviously arisen in his mind and unsettled him. Machaneka realized this was probably a good time to leave him alone. She walked past him and out of the back door to check out the mineral garden and see the detached bedroom.

When Machaneka walked into the mineral garden, a wave of tranquility rushed over her. It felt as wonderful as her own Sacred Garden, and it did not disappoint visually. She was expecting to see a large variety of various crystals and formations. She was correct except that some of the crystals and formations were huge. The mineral garden had crystals everywhere that looked like they were growing from the ground.

They had the appearance of blooms everywhere. A five-foot- tall amethyst was in the center of the yard with various shades of purple veins running through it. Smaller clusters of amethysts were surrounding it, glistening and beautiful.

There were carnelian, jasper, pyrite, quartz, jade, hematite, and several other plots that had small to large stones all over them, some sporadic and some that looked specifically placed. All in all, it was a sight to see. Machaneka was honored that Trevelyn trusted her enough to leave her and her companions alone in her home for who knows how long. She made sure to stay on the stone lined path that led to the detached bedroom as she walked to the other end of the mineral garden to see it. With every step she took, she felt the energies of the various crystals. It was an amazing feeling; she felt like she was being recharged without even trying to rejuvenate.

When she opened the door to the detached bedroom, she stopped to take in what she saw. This "detached bedroom" was a sanctuary to behold. Green, gold, red, white, and yellow tapestries, pillows everywhere, an altar covered in healing stones with glittering rhinestones covering the candleholders, a chandelier made of abalone shells, onyx, and what looked like diamonds, sparkled and glistened from the ceiling. A large jade egg sat atop the small table next to the bed. That is when she saw Prentice. Letting out a small gasp, Machaneka was once again caught off guard by how beautiful he was.

Prentice had taken off his shirt and was sitting on the bed with his legs crossed underneath him meditating. The deep caramel color of his skin and his well-chiseled arms and chest appeared to glow by the light of the candles in the room. He looked to be in a state of complete peace. Machaneka wanted to touch him, but she didn't dare. She stared at the companion that the Sacred Council had sent to assist her. He was as mysterious to her as he was beautiful. At every turn she found he had another gift, another power, another ability that she didn't know about. She still had no idea exactly what his role was for the Sacred Council, or even where he came from or had been. He seemed to know everything about her, and just about everything that she had come up against.

His meeting Trevelyn was the first time that he was unaware who he was dealing with. Machaneka remembered that they both showed a high level of reverence for one another once Trevelyn allowed him to read her, taking note that for once, he had to be allowed to do so.

With anyone else he just scanned them without them knowing. Seeing him at peace was comforting. Since they had joined together as a team, he was always holding a part of himself back, prepared for defense if necessary. At this moment, the combination of his beauty, strength, and mystique was almost intoxicating. He was the only male that she had felt anything for besides Jerod, or rather Shaju, and she still wasn't quite sure what she felt. Machaneka's inquisitive mind began to wander and wonder. She was pulled from her revelry by the sound of his voice.

"No wonder you stay within an inch of trouble, you think too much for a spirit warrior." Prentice extended his hand for her to join him on the bed.

Machaneka accepted his assistance to be seated next to him and replied with a small laugh. "I guess you can say that. To the chagrin of Chango especially, I am always possibly heading towards unnecessary danger because I'm always thinking about how I feel."

Prentice heard the confusion in her statement clearly. He felt like now was the perfect time to share a couple of things with her. "Spirits feel, Machaneka, that is why people connect so intrinsically. Without spirit in them they would not be able to connect. In your case, it's not that you feel that is problematic, it's the possibility of you not separating your feelings from what you've been chosen to do. It really is OK for you to be who you are, that is what makes you so magnificent. That is what makes you so maddeningly beautiful, that you feel so deeply.

Don't be ashamed or worried, it is probably your greatest superpower to say the least." Machaneka lowered her head as she listened to him. Prentice reached out and touched her chin, raising her head up to face him. His touch sent waves of electricity through her. Now she was nervous. Prentice continued to speak. "You are not the first to wonder about or want to have a full human experience. You are one of the first who is as powerful as you are, but not solely the first. When you assume a body, you are just as much human as you are spirit warrior. Most others do not possess the capacity to be equal.

They are primarily spirit warriors using a vessel. You treat your vessel like it belongs to you. That is admirable. There was another spirit warrior who longed for the opportunity to share a life with someone in the flesh. That warrior also wanted to feel love and be loved. His decision to ascend to full spirit warrior was not an easy nor painless one for him to make. The Council wasn't certain until he accepted, if he would be able to overcome his attachment to having a normal human experience with a woman that he desperately loved. I believe that you may know him by the name of Shaju."

Machaneka began to tremble slightly. How did he know Jerod, her precious Shaju? How did he know his story? Prentice nodded his head while looking into her eyes. "I know, and for the record, after spending the time that I have spent with you, I not only know but I understand. He was able to accept full ascension but not without the condition that whenever you needed him, he would be allowed to come to you. The fact that the Sacred Council made that allowance for him speaks volumes to not only how much they value him but also you. You, Machaneka, are a very special warrior. The depth of it all is not for me to reveal but time will bear it for you. The things that you would like to know about me will also be revealed to you when the time is right. That time is not now. For now, just understand that I will accompany, serve, and protect you with everything that I have, and that is more than you can imagine or fathom right now. And to answer the question that was in your head while I was meditating, yes, I could and would love you if we were humans sharing an experience together. Love is all powerful and transcends spiritual and human boundaries. I love you now and have no qualms about it."

Machaneka closed her eyes and inhaled deeply. Prentice kissed her on the forehead and put on his shirt. He rose from the bed and walked to the door. "I believe it is time for us to join Phillip for some of whatever that magnificent smell is for dinner." Her head was swirling with thoughts as she looked up at Prentice, illuminated by the early moonlight standing in the doorway. She gathered herself and got off the bed to walk with him back into the cottage. When they walked through the back door into the kitchen, Phillip was standing over the dining table that he had set elegantly, complete with flowers in a vase from the garden in the front yard. "I do believe I have outdone myself if I may say so. Your timing is perfect, dinner is ready, and I am actually hungry. Please have a seat."

Prentice pulled a chair out for Machaneka then sat down himself. The plates were clear glass with gold rims, and they sat atop purple chargers that had gold leafing running through them. The linens were lavender, and the napkin holders were white and gold with a small citrine in the center of them. Prentice poured water from a crystal pitcher into exquisitely carved crystal water glasses whilePhillip began preparing plates. Prentice looked around the kitchen and said, "If I was one to bet, my wager would be that Trevelyn has a favorite color, and it is purple."

Machaneka laughed. "If you were a betting man you would be a bet richer today. Her favorite color, unlike her locations, past times, and crystal collections, has never changed. It has always been purple and always will be. Quite befitting of her, to love a color so rich and royal."

Phillip walked over to the table with a plate of food for each of them. When he turned around to fix his plate, Prentice and Machaneka looked in amazement at what had been placed before them. Phillip had prepared roasted crab, red lentils, milk rice, curried beetroot, and a pennywort salad. The aromas from the curry and fresh roasted crab floated from their plates. Phillip came to the table with his plate and then told them that he was a little rusty, but he had done his best with what he could find and remember. "Nonsense!" Machaneka and Prentice responded in unison.

"This food looks delicious, Machaneka added, "and thank you for such an extravagant meal!" They each blessed their food in silence and then began to eat. The food was so good that Machaneka almost screamed! Prentice went to work on his crab and occasionally glanced at Phillip shaking his head.

"This is ridiculous, Phillip! You've been a chef all of this time and we could've partaken together well before now!" Phillip was humbled and satisfied seeing them devour his food with so much appreciation. They continued to eat in silence until they all were just sitting there with nothing left on their plates. Machaneka told Phillip to go get some rest and that she would clean the dishes.

Phillip responded quickly. "You will not need to persuade me about that one. Good night, all!"

Prentice and Machaneka cleared the table, and she began washing the dishes in a pot of hot water from the stove. When she was finished, Prentice helped her to put all of the dishes away. Then he turned to her and said, "Sleep well, Warrior Queen. Tomorrow will hopefully bring you what we came here for." Machaneka told him thank you. She could still feel the kiss he placed on her forehead, so she dared not speak too much and complicate anything. Prentice laughed as he was walking out of the back door to the detached bedroom. As she was leaving the kitchen, she heard him say, "Well done, Queen. We have enough to deal with as it is."

Machaneka went into the peacock-themed bedroom down the hall, took off her clothing and got into the bed. Before she knew it, she was headed into a deep sleep.

Trevelyn had just opened her eyes to see that she was sitting under the moonlit sky. Hours had passed and she now knew what she needed to do. She rose from the base of the tree and put her robing back on, carefully tying and securing it so that she could move easily and quickly through the trail that would take her back to her home. She was satisfied in knowing that she now had something to offer Machaneka. She was a bit unsure whether or not it would be received with a full understanding and acceptance. She moved effortlessly from the spot that she had been seated in for hours. Her legs after all of that time only required a few moments of stretching before she was able to go home. When she walked through the door the aromas from the dinner Phillip had prepared greeted her. She smiled, turned down the hallway, and headed to her bedroom. She went inside and got into her bed. Within a few minutes she too was in a deep, dreamless sleep.

The next morning Trevelyn heard her guests moving about her home. She did not join them; she would meet with them later in the living room and share what she had for Machaneka. For now, she needed to move the many boxes, bags, and clothing items in the closet out of her way. She needed to get to her safe. Once she opened it, she retrieved a small ornate box. She placed the box in her pocket and then left out of her bedroom. Trevelyn walked down the hallway and into the living room where Machaneka and Phillip were sitting side by side enjoying a cup of tea. She smiled at them in acknowledgement of their presence and then went over to the fireplace. She began to sort through the ashes from the last fire that she burned with her hands then she removed the small box from her pocket and placed it on the hearth in front of the fireplace. Every now and then, she would pick something out of the ashes and place it in the small box. Machaneka and Phillip did not try to engage her in conversation or ask any questions. Trevelyn was obviously very focused on whatever it was that she was digging around for in the ashes. Meanwhile, Prentice was standing in the window of the detached bedroom looking out into the mineral garden in the back yard. He had been many places that held different energies, some good and some not so good, but what he was feeling in that moment was different. He was amazed at the beauty of the crystals in their raw form and even more intriguing was the pull that he felt from them just being in the same vicinity. This was unchartered territory for him, and it was refreshing to encounter something new.

As the sun shone through the window on his skin, he was more relaxed and comfortable than he had been in a long time. He thought about his conversation with Machaneka and wondered if he had given her too much information to process or if he should have waited. He accepted that what he had shared was truth, and if a spirit warrior of the second sentry for the Sacred Council of the universe couldn't handle truth, then no one could. He was trying to put it out of his mind, to stop thinking about her, but it seemed like he could not. He laughed to himself, shook his head, and said, "If you can't beat them, join them!"

Prentice walked into the living from having come from the detached bedroom with a smile on his face. Machaneka and Phillip greeted him and then he sat down on the loveseat adjacent to the sofa. He joined them in watching Trevelyn moving and rearranging ashes repeatedly, and occasionally pulling something out that they could not see and place it in a small box.

Hours had passed and the afternoon sun was filtering into the living room. The temperature in the cottage had begun to rise as well. Suddenly, Trevelyn stood up and said, "It's getting warm in here, let me open some windows so that we can get the ocean breeze flowing through." Finally, the ice was broken. The three visitors exhaled almost at the same time. They had been patiently sitting and trying not to do or say anything that might be disruptive to Trevelyn's process. Trevelyn walked from room to room opening the windows of the home. Then she went into her bedroom and changed her clothes. When she rejoined them, she had on a pair of jeans and a tank top. Her dreadlocks had been released from the bun that held them so beautifully together and she was barefoot.

Trevelyn took a seat on a large lavender floor pillow that was embroidered in gold and white threads with a crown on it. She got herself into a comfortable position and then addressed Machaneka. "I have a couple of things for you, and I have something to tell you. Would you like for me to go ahead, or should we speak in private?"

Prentice and Phillip rose to their feet to give preparing to leave the room so that they could speak in private, but Machaneka held her hand up for them to stop. "Please, share what you have found. I would like for them to see as well."

Trevelyn looked at her and opened the small box that she had been placing things in while she was digging around in the ashes of her fireplace. "Hold out your hand." Machaneka moved closer to Trevelyn and did what she had been instructed to do. Trevelyn poured seven stones out into Machaneka's hand. Machaneka felt a surge go through her from head to toe. Then she stared into her palm at the stones. They were beyond beautiful, and she had never seen anything like them before. Trevelyn allowed her a moment to take in the magnificence of what she was holding.

Phillip looked into Machaneka's hand and then spoke very quietly. "For centuries upon centuries I have seen royalty from ancient times to modern times wearing the most extravagant and exquisite gems that anyone could ever lay eyes upon. I have never seen anything as beautiful as these anywhere."

Trevelyn smiled, looking at Machaneka who was patiently waiting to hear what she was supposed to do with them. "After much meditation and prayer, it was revealed to me that your Beloved Elder Odara is gravely ill. I was told when I moved into this cottage by the previous owner who was also a lightworker and healer to never clean the ashes out of the fireplace. She told me that when the time came, I would need them. So, for years I have never touched that fireplace other than to burn a fire to charge the crystals that can be charged by fire.

When I finished my meditation, I did not have an answer for you yet, but as I made my way back home, I knew instinctively that what I needed was in the ashes that I was told to never clean away. The stones that I am giving you are not of this place, but they spoke to me as I gathered them. I have given you seven dark green jade stones. In the center of each of them is a sapphire. Surrounding each sapphire are rare diamonds with the highest of frequency. Jade is known to help the body heal itself and it strengthens the heart, kidneys, eyes, and immune system. Sapphire restores balance within the body and aligns physical, mental, and spiritual planes. Lastly, but definitely not the least, diamonds strengthen and re-energize the energy centers of the wearer. They radiate at a high frequency and open all chakra channels while giving out positive healing properties. You will find that all of the stones have been drilled with a small hole. You need to make a head piece that incorporates two of them. The piece should fit her head so that one of them rests on top of her head and the other one hangs on her forehead where the third eye chakra is located between the eyes. With the other five you need to make a body chain and spread them out so that they align with the other chakra centers of her body. This is not all that you need to do. What I need to say to you next may be problematic considering the nature of your current journeys through your past."

    Prentice braced himself to support Machaneka. Trevelyn was going to tell her what he hadn't been able to when she interrupted him in a prior conversation. Phillip sat on the edge of sofa waiting to hear what she was going to say. He wasn't accustomed to humans being aware of what to do in situations involving spirit warriors. Machaneka knew that whatever Trevelyn said, she wasn't going to like it. She looked Trevelyn in the eye and said, "Tell me."

Trevelyn lowered her head for a moment and then returned her gaze to face Machaneka. "The sacred and blessed stones that I have given you are not enough. They will be of great assistance for her healing process but none of it will matter unless you give her a part of yourself. You will need to breathe the fire that you were created from into her, and it will restore her to the point that she can overcome what she is battling."

"Well, that's easy!" Machaneka responded quickly. And then she saw the look on Phillip, Prentice, and Trevelyn's faces. Alarmed, she raised her voice. "What's wrong? What am I missing?"

Prentice took her by the hand and began to explain. "You are a spirit blessed with mighty gifts from the Sacred Council. If you give the elder some of the fire that you were created from, you will be sharing a part of your grace because it is not yours fully to give. Along with that, if you do so, then our journey for you to make the decision to ascend higher or not will be over, because once you share that part of you, you will no longer have the divinity that allows you to transcend higher. In short, you will remain forever a warrior for the second sentry, never again having the opportunity to be promoted or grow any further. You have an enormous decision to make."

Machaneka sat looking down at the stones in her hand with tears streaming down her face. She thought after the Sacred Council came and offered her the promotion to full ascension that it was the most important decision she would ever have to make. She was wrong. The decision to save the elder Odara and remain at the level she was at now forever or allow nature to take its natural course and still be in a position to ascend fully was a whole different level of decision making. She looked at Prentice and Phillip and asked, "If the elder dies, will the body I inhabit as Odara also expire?"

Prentice answered her slowly. "She will not expire because before you transition to full ascension, her body will be touched by each member of the Sacred Council as a tribute to the last vessel that you resided in."

Machaneka spoke through clenched teeth. "And if I choose not to ascend?"

"Then she will survive because you will be the life force that drives her- forever," Phillip responded. Machaneka couldn't believe what she was hearing. She stood up and said, "Take me to her!" Phillip and Prentice stood up and said in unison, "No!"

Trevelyn stood and took her friend by the hand. "You cannot fix everything, Machaneka. Everything happens in its own time. You need to get back to the journey that you were on. The third moon will be gracing you when you release the time hold that you used to come here."

Machaneka was so hurt, angry, and confused that her palms began to smolder. Trevelyn snatched her hand back. "Ouch!" Realizing what she had done, Machaneka began apologizing profusely. "Oh my goodness, I am so sorry! Please forgive me. I would never—"

"I know you wouldn't," Trevelyn interrupted her. "I love you. Go be amazing and make your decision wisely. Just remember that there is no wrong answer. It comes down to whatever you do is exactly what you were supposed to do." Then she turned to Phillip and Prentice. "Gentlemen, it has been an absolute pleasure. I hope my home afforded you rest and comfort." Trevelyn headed to the front door where she grabbed an intricately carved ebony walking stick and then walked out of the front door.

Realizing that Machaneka was in a partial state of shock, Prentice and Phillip took control over the next moment. They each put an arm around Machaneka and then joined hands. "We call on the wind to return us to the course that we deviated from. Take us to Mount Huayna Picchu." The roomwas without sound for a minute or two and the soundof tribal drums came thundering in. The cottagebecame a blur as the wind swooped in and surrounded the trio. In the blink of an eye, they wereairborne and moving swiftly to their next destination.

We do not remember days we remember moments

5
The Third Moon

Mount Huayna in the Andes mountains was a very beautiful place. At the foot of it was the historically and culturally rich city of Macchu Picchu built by the Incas in Peru. The mountain itself wasn't one of the largest in the world but it was a spectacular site. What made it important for Machaneka to visit, were the four angels who lived on the mountaintop near the ancient Temple of The Moon. The mountain was lush and was the home of many different types of foliage and flowers. Orchids and begonias, along with a vast number of trees and wildlife graced the mountain. The angels that lived amongst this beauty were charged with very important assignments. They each had several sets of silver wings, and the silver haired angels were the best of friends. They flew daily, year-round amongst the trees consulting with one another and arguing over who should get what. They listened when the trees spoke to the wind and got excited when the birds brought them messages. During tourist season when people were on excursions, they took to the treetops and watched as thousands of people tried to hike the mountain. They never rested though; their job would not allow for it. Dalin, Jamer, Sani, and Jerifenn were responsible for assigning unborn children grace, humility, and wisdom while they were in the womb. They were excitedly flittering back and forth between two sacred Pisonay trees when the wind swooped in and placed Phillip, Prentice, and Machaneka in their midst.

Phillip was excited to get Machaneka to this visit. He knew that she needed something positive to distract her from the situation involving the two Odaras. He was hoping that the comical, always in motion angels would make her feel better. As they settled onto the ground, unbeknownst to the angels, the moon was beginning to rise above them. Machaneka looked up and saw the moon beginning to shine. It was the third moon of her journey. Prentice admired the new full moon for a moment and then pointed towards the four angels. "I think you will appreciate this, Machaneka." She turned to see what he was pointing out to her. Jamer, the oldest of the four was hovering over an enormous flower that was about four feet wide. Jamer was brown skinned, shorter than the others and slightly on the plump side. Her hair was a lively crown of long silver curled locs that framed a small face with eyes that were always smiling.

"Look, Jerifenn! She's still growing!" Jerifenn, who was petite and medium build with golden brown skin and radiant eyes that held many stories, ran her fingers through her short silver afro then flew over to Jamer's side and was obviously excited and ecstatic as well. Dalin, the tallest of the four, came over to see what the fuss was about. She stood almost a foot taller than the other three; her silver crown of soft curls framed a face that held a dimpled smile that always made you think she was on the verge of laughing.

Sani, who was the smallest in build but definitely not character, came right behind Dalin and put her hand over heart. Sani's long silver braids hung down her back and were a striking contrast to her ebony-colored skin. Sani always had the look of serenity and peace on her face, even when excited. "How beautiful!" They all flittered from one side of the flower to the other.

Dalin stared at the flower and said, "Who was this again?"

Sani laughed before Jerifenn answered her. "Who was this? Are you serious?" "There are so many, I forget sometimes," Dalin said. Jamer put her hands on her hips in midair. "This is one of the most important blooms we've ever had," she said. "This type of bloom only comes every few million years. Really, Dalin, you should get your memory reset! This bloom marked the creation of that spirit warrior into flesh for the first time- Machaneka, the one that we were so excited about."

"Ohhhh, that's right, the pretty one with all of the planetary and star alignment, the fire girl!"

Sani laughed again as Jerifenn shook her head. "The fire girl, that's funny, Dalin." "I wonder how far she has come along, Jerifenn added. "Obviously she's still getting stronger and growing, quite quickly I might add. This flower was half this size not long ago." Jamer clapped her hands and said, "Let's check on the other one that shook us up a bit. It's not as big as this one but I wonder if it's flourishing as well."

The four angels took flight; Phillip, Machaneka, and Prentice did so as well. They flew to another spot a few miles higher up and Jamer got excited again. "Well, look at there! She's not as big but definitely close in beauty." Jerifenn, Dalin, and Sani joined their friend and marveled at the second huge bloom whose rows of petals had spread to almost two feet across.

"And this one is?" Dalin asked again.

Jerifenn looked and Sani, and Sani looked at Jamer who was slightly agitated now. "This one is Odara," Jamer explained. "The one that YOU insisted on extra grace for, Dalin! My goodness, I can't believe you sometimes!"

Dalin remembered well once Jamer said the name. She had felt immediately when the bloom began to form that Odara was special and would face a series of trials and complicated situations. Jerifenn had given her a hefty dose of wisdom, Jamer gave her an incredible sense of humor, and Sani insisted on humility in depth. The angels fluttered back and forth reminiscing and arguing over whose gift was the most important.

Machaneka was stunned. She was also amused at the four silver-haired, beautiful, winged women and the way that they communicated with one another. Grandmothers. That's what they reminded her of.

Grandmothers who would bake and trade recipes then compare the results. Phillip laughed aloud as they began to fuss about who was responsible for the new blooms that they saw that morning. Prentice was still watching Machaneka intently. "Bet you had no idea that your birth was marked by a rare bloom." "That's a bet you would've won," she responded. "And I thought the Sacred Council did all of this." Phillip joined the conversation. "At one time they did. But as the world continued to grow, they began to delegate responsibilities. These amazing creatures that we're watching have had a hand in many millions of blessings over time. They are a special crew."

Machaneka watched them in awe and admiration and then exclaimed, "They said that Odara was a special bloom as well and that she's still growing! That has to mean something!"

Prentice and Phillip looked at one another and Phillip patted her on the shoulder. "Perhaps so, Machaneka. They did say it was still growing."

For the next few days Phillip, Prentice, and Machaneka followed the foursome in flight all over the mountain as they attended to new blooms, assigned attributes, and bickered while they laughed at one another. Machaneka had taken a special liking to Jerifenn. She was no nonsense but had a sense of humor that seemed to settle the others when necessary. She appeared to be sweet. A bit quiet and very intelligent. She was adamant about the difference between wisdom and knowledge and that there be a definite balance when she was deciding what to impart into the blooms. Machaneka noticed that the other three angels also seemed to be partial to her. At one point when she was watching Jerifenn move about a small bloom, she thought she saw Jerifenn look in her direction and wink at her. That couldn't be though, they were veiled and only there for observation. She was sure Jerifenn couldn't see her. Or at least sure that she wasn't supposed to be able to.

During the course of their visit, Machaneka learned quite a bit about herself and how she came to be. It was quite interesting hearing the angels discuss her as they went back to see her bloom every day. What was even more exciting, was hearing them speak about her beloved Odara. Things were beginning to add up for her about why she was so drawn to her and fond of her. It was beginning to feel like they were kindreds. So many things were running through her mind, and always in the back of her mind was the question she didn't have an answer for yet. What was she going to do about the elder Odara? Prentice approached her with a smile and said, "Still thinking, huh? Well, you can table those thoughts for now. We must get you to your next destination for the fourth moon, and it's not as pretty as what you've witnessed here. As a matter of fact, I'm not looking forward to it. The place we're headed changes the mindset of those who've been there. I trust that you can handle it, but it may be unsettling a bit."

"Where are we headed, Prentice?" Machaneka asked. Phillip appeared by the side of Prentice and responded for him. "To the containment realm, my dear, specifically to the banishment sector where everyone that you have ever defeated that wasn't destroyed now resides. I'm sure they will sense your presence and not be pleased at all." Machaneka wanted to see what the angels were doing one last time. She had no idea what the containment realm was like, and what Phillip and Prentice had said made her feel uncomfortable. She wasn't the least bit worried about anyone or anything that she had already defeated. She wanted to see what the angels were up to one last time before she left the mountain.

Jamer, Dalin, and Sani were bustling about the trees checking and scanning the perimeter of the mountain for new blooms. It took her a moment to see Jerifenn. She finally spotted her with her back to them tending to the area around Odara's bloom. Machaneka wondered what she was doing. Phillip and Prentice had turned their attention to the other three angels who had suddenly become very excited. "Another spirit warrior! It's been over a thousand years, something good is in the making!" Jamer was clapping her hands as she exclaimed about the bloom she had just found.

Phillip took flight towards her instantly saying, "I'd like to witness this exchange; they are quite fascinating these three." Prentice took flight right behind him in their direction saying, "So would I!" Machaneka did not move. She was fixated on trying to see what Jerifenn was doing around the bloom that marked the arrival of Odara. Jerifenn on the other hand, did not stop what she was doing to join her counterparts although she had to have heard them clearly. Machaneka arose from her spot to hover a little, thinking she could get a better view. Then Jerifenn did something that took her breath away. Jerifenn flew over the center of the flower and collected pollen from the anther of the bloom, then she came back to the ground and got on her knees. Bent over she raised up the top petals of the flower and then plucked one of the lower petals. Her next move was what astounded Machaneka. Jerifenn took one of the brightly colored sashes from around her waist and placed the petal covered in the pollen from the bloom in it, and then she raised up the sash, kissed it, and let it fly free in the wind. The sash flew directly to where Machaneka stood. Machaneka looked at Jerifenn who had bowed her head and flew away to join her friends near the newly discovered bloom. Knowing that she wasn't supposed to interact with anyone for any reason during her travels,

Machaneka hesitated, but only for a moment. Looking to be sure that Phillip and Prentice were engrossed with the other four angels, she picked the sash up from the ground and tucked it into the bosom of her gown. She realized that earlier during their visit when she thought Jerifenn had winked at her that had been correct. And now Jerifenn had given her a gift. Something directly related to Odara. She was thrilled, and she composed herself right on time for Phillip and Prentice to rejoin her.

They came back to where she was, and Phillip cleared his throat. "Now, after all of that love and goodness, we shall head to the containment realm."

Choices are the hinges of destiny

6
The Fourth Moon

Machaneka, Phillip, and Prentice emerged from the portal to the containment realm. Instantly she felt the weight of the darkness and turmoil. The containment realm was the place where the evils of the universe, or rather the conduits for the evils of the universe were sent to spend eternity once they had been conquered by spirit warriors. In some religions it would be the perfect description for Hell. Because they weren't created by the Sacred Council, they couldn't be stripped of their evil powers by them. They could only be held in a place that was powerful enough to contain and restrict them from using them. The realm was heavily cloaked and protected to prevent entrance and escape from anyone or anything that wasn't sent by the Sacred Council. No one knew where the entry to the realm was and there was only one portal that could get you there. To go through the portal, you needed a series of numbers and chants that had to be requested from the Sacred Council. Once you completed the sequence correctly, the Sacred Council sent a message to the keeper of containment realm who opened the portal. If you did not instantly come through the portal it closed, and the process would have to be repeated.

The keeper of the containment realm was an ex-spirit warrior who had been retired by the Sacred Council for breaking a sacred oath. The severity of her actions usually was one of the few that could cause the termination of the life of a spirit warrior. She had been spared from that consequence by the grace of Bitol. So instead of losing her life, she was banished from the heavens and assigned to be the keeper of the containment realm, where she would forever be responsible for the security of the realm where the most evil and hideous perpetrators from the universe resided miserably. The keeper's name was Jonaraja, and perfectly befitting was the meaning of her name – "a secret keeper."

Jonaraja was a tall, strong-looking female figure. Her jet-black hair was a mane of spiral curls. She had an attractive face, but it had long lost its shine and her smile. Cloaked in a dark grey robe with a black hood, she patrolled the cells before greeting her guests. She hated the job that she had been assigned to spare her life. She was forced to live here in exile doing one of the most important jobs in the universe while being surrounded by the stench of evil and the constant wailing of the captured and or defeated.

Once excited about her assignment because she understood the importance of it, Jonaraja was now bitter and disgusted. Centuries of time had passed, and she no longer could rely on the memories of her previous life to afford her something to smile about. She had begun to despise the call of the Sacred

Council to open the portal to receive yet another miserable soulless entity into the realm and now she had to open the portal for Machaneka, Phillip, and Prentice so that Machaneka could see what she had helped to rid the universe of. Jonaraja almost snarled. Machaneka. It had seemed that over the last few years the most notorious and powerful of the captured entities who were sent to the realm were the result of having lost a battle to Machaneka. Jonaraja envied her. She should have been the one to win so much favor from the Sacred Council through victorious battle against evil. Instead, she was stuck in this God-forsaken realm to monitor the madness and chaos of the defeated as she patrolled the cells encased in protective orbs.

Despite all of the angst that Jonaraja held, she also had a secret of her own. For hundreds of years, she had been extracting a small amount of power from each of the inhabitants of the realm during the small window of time that it took to transfer them from a transport orb to their cell. Jonaraja had managed to become quite powerful from the energies that she had extracted. She also had become more and more hateful as the evils that she collected were absorbed into her spirit willingly. This visit from the almighty Machaneka was not going to be just a viewing as she and her companions thought. Jonaraja was going to overcome Machaneka while she was in the realm where her powers were useless and escape from the realm of doom with Machaneka's spirit and her power. She was certain that her companions would be of no issue. They couldn't possibly be a match for what she had acquired. At least that is what she believed.

As Jonaraja approached Machaneka, Phillip, and Prentice, Machaneka had a faint memory of seeing her in the ranks somewhere before she had taken her first human form. Jonaraja greeted them and held her arm out to show them the way towards the banishment cells. Phillip was taking in the dark, sullen appearance of who he remembered as a raving beauty. It was sad for him to see what she had been fated to. Prentice was alarmed. Something about the indifference in her greeting set off several red flags. Of course, that could easily be attributed to having to exist in a land of nothing but horrible energy, but he felt like it was more than that. He watched her closely as she moved, noticing that whenever Machaneka was close to her in stride, that she almost seemed to recoil – like a cobra. This was not good. There was going to be trouble, he could sense it, and Machaneka and Phillip were oblivious to what he was feeling. Prentice mentally prepared himself for battle. He would protect Machaneka at all costs, even at the cost of destroying the keeper of the containment realm. He made sure to mask himself so that Jonaraja wouldn't pick up on his concern.

They all walked as Jonaraja led them through the dark barren land of nothing until she came to a halt. She stretched her arms out before her and an enormous, bolted doorway materialized in front of them. Jonaraja produced a key from inside of her cloak and unlocked the door. She pushed the door open and stepped aside for her guests to enter. Machaneka, Phillip, and Prentice all walked through the doorway and Jonaraja stepped in after them and closed the door, locking it from the inside. They were standing in a dark hallway, cold and drafty. After they had walked for some time down the hallway, Jonaraja turned to them and said, "Prepare yourselves. When I open this next door, the energy is tangible." She produced another key from her cloak and held it up in the dark. Another door materialized and she unlocked it. As soon as they stepped through the door Machaneka felt the presence of evil.

Prentice stepped in front of Machaneka so that he was in between her and Jonaraja. Machaneka was caught off guard and startled a little. As they walked down the corridor that held the cells, the sound of hissing and growling was the first thing that they heard. The closer they got to the cells the louder the sound of misery was around them. The first cell that they approached held what had the appearance of a small built elderly man. He was sitting in a chair with his legs crossed. Machaneka recognized him immediately. He was the first being that she had sent to the containment realm. His appearance was deceiving; in actuality, he was an eight feet tall, maniacal demon. The body that he was using when he was banished was the one that he would be trapped in forever. That fact did not change nor alter his capacity to destroy and kill.

When Machaneka was called to go into warfare with him, he had almost obliterated an entire section of the spirit realm, taking the souls of everything he destroyed and regurgitating them back into life as minions who would serve him. She remembered clearly how close she had come to almost being defeated by him in her inexperience with battling demons.

Phillip wondered what the old man he was looking at could have done to get sent to the banishment realm. No sooner than that thought crossed his mind the demon looked in their direction and let out a blood curdling howl. Jonaraja stepped in front of the cell and said, "They all now know that you are here. Let's move swiftly, it will be a long night for me when you leave." Machaneka didn't respond to her. She turned and followed behind Prentice as they went further down the corridor. They passed hundreds of cells, their inhabitants snarling, hissing, growling, and screaming. Some of them yelled obscenities and threats to Machaneka. All of them were rapidly becoming enraged.

As they walked and came upon the various cells, Machaneka remembered each and every one of them vividly. She remembered the battles, the spells, the injuries, and the rescues. It made her proud to be who she was and made her sick to her stomach to have to see her enemies again. When they reached the end of the corridor, she had revisited over one hundred monstrous, evil beings. She was ready to leave this place. Jonaraja turned to face them and said, "I have shown you what the Sacred Council wanted you to see. We will head back a different route so that you don't have to see them again."

Jonaraja turned to walk away with Prentice behind her, and Machaneka in between Phillip and Prentice. Halfway through their trek back to the doorway, Jonaraja stopped and began to clutch her abdomen. Machaneka stepped in front of Prentice and reached for her while asking if she was alright. This was Jonaraja's opportunity, she only needed a touch from Machaneka to assume her body. Unfortunately for her and fortunately for Machaneka, Prentice had seen it coming. Before they had begun their descent to return to the doorway, Prentice had assumed the image of Machaneka and cloaked her in his image. Machaneka was unaware that he had done so. She only thought they had switched places in walking position. She didn't see him as herself ahead of her, she only saw him walking behind Jonaraja. When Jonaraja tried to extract what she thought was the fire from Machaneka's spirit, she was horrified when Machaneka wrapped a ring of fire around her throat and pulled it tight.

As she struggled, she was confused because Machaneka should be powerless in this realm. Absolutely no one could bring their powers into the realm lest they be tempted to assist any of the prisoners in escape. Her confusion was quickly quelled as the image of Machaneka dissipated and she saw that it was her companion Prentice who had a deathlock on her throat. Machaneka cried out and tried to move towards them, but Phillip had already moved and held up his hands in front of her.

"Stay out of the way, Machaneka!" She listened to Phillip but didn't quite understand what was happening. Why had Prentice attacked the keeper? The answer to her question began to reveal itself as the evils that Jonaraja had been collecting began to merge together in an effort to save the body of their host. Jonaraja sprouted horns and fangs, and venomous snakes slithered from under her cloak and tried to attack Prentice. His death grip did not waiver.

"You dare try to assassinate a spirit warrior for the Sacred Council of the universe in my presence!" Prentice was livid, and as Machaneka stood with Phillip blocking her she watched him magnify in size as his wings began to spread and rise. His lower body was girded with a sword, dagger, and a bow and arrow. Prentice lifted into the air with the quickly dying Jonaraja.

As they began to rise, Prentice threw his head back and exclaimed in a roar, "Take us to the surface!" Before they could blink, they were all on the surface of the realm and Prentice was airborne with Jonaraja. It was at this point that Machaneka realized that Prentice had just saved her life. She was angry, relieved, and shaken. Phillip was livid.

It was the first time ever that the Sacred Council had ever sent him somewhere that danger could be imminent. Now airborne, Prentice was choking the life out of Jonaraja with the fire he had stolen from Machaneka when he kissed her on her forehead at Trevelyn's home. "I know that you thought she would be powerless in your realm and that you would actually succeed.

You were correct about Machaneka being powerless in your realm. My power, however, is magnified in any spiritual realm that I enter. I am not a spirit warrior, I am all that is and all that will be. My power only falls short of the capacity of God himself. Your plan to kill me and Machaneka, and lock Phillip the messenger for the Sacred Council in that deplorable realm is unforgivable. You have broken yet another oath to serve and this time it will cost you your life."

Prentice snatched the cord of fire from around her neck and hurled her into the stratosphere. He produced a sphere and threw it in the same direction. It made contact with Jonaraja and then encapsulated her body. He withdrew his sword and cut the fire cord in half. Then he withdrew the bow and used the fire cord as an arrow. "It is fire that you wanted, so it is fire that you will get!" Prentice shot the fire cord into the sphere where it hit Jonaraja directly in her heart. Her body exploded into flames, and she screamed with the last breath that she had. While her body burned, Prentice watched as the evil energies that she had been collecting in her spirit released into total mayhem inside of the sphere and then began to burn in the fire that consumed their host. When the last wail had subsided and there wasn't even a trace of an ash, Prentice threw his dagger into the sphere and it collapsed without a trace. He raised his hand, and the dagger came back to him, with the cord of fire wrapped around it. "So be it!" he declared aloud and then raised his wings once more in flight and headed back to the surface of the containment realm where Machaneka and Phillip were waiting.

When Prentice landed next to them Machaneka was spellbound. He was radiating a power that she had never witnessed. He reminded her of her beloved Shaju, who she had last seen as Jerod in Odara's home. Prentice removed his dagger and unwound the fire cord from it. "I believe this belongs to you," he said as he handed it to her and lowered his wings.

"How did you get this?" Machaneka asked him. "I stole it from a forehead kiss." They stood face to face in silent conversation and Phillip interrupted.

"I don't know what's going on here, and I probably shouldn't concern myself with it. Matters of the heart aren't quite my cup of tea. I do know, however, that we have a journey to make. Oh, and that I am forever indebted to you, Master Prentice. Forever indeed. Shall we move on?" Prentice and Machaneka were locked in a gaze but Machaneka answered him. "Yes, we shall. I am ready, Phillip."

7
The Fifth Moon

After leaving the containment realm, Machaneka didn't even bother to ask where they were headed next. She was still reeling from what could have been an attack on her life, and the telepathic conversation that she had with Prentice. Once they went back through the portal, she was quiet as their wind chariot enveloped them and whisked them away. When they placed on the ground and the wind stopped swirling, she looked at her surroundings and almost screamed. They were standing in front of Odara's chateau in the South of France.

She faced Phillip with questions in her eyes. He simply smiled and said, "The fifth moon is upon us and there are things that will happen here that may make or break your decision. I suggest you begin with a visit to the elder Odara. You may want to channel her before going to visit. An abrupt pop up may be too much for her in her fragile state. I am headed to the back patio to enjoy some of that delicious Oolong tea that Mutora enjoys with me." Phillip walked away towards the house as Machaneka and Prentice stood in the courtyard. Prentice offered her his harm. "Shall we, Mademoiselle?" Machaneka put her arm through his. "I believe we shall."

They walked up to the front porch where Mutora and Roma were standing with the door open smiling. Mutora saw that the journey had a profound impact on Machaneka. The spirit warrior had grown at least two more inches of hair and her chocolate-colored skin was flawless. In taking in the sight of her, Mutora realized that the difference was not really in her physical appearance. Machaneka was wearing her power. She had grown as a spirit. Roma stepped aside so that Machaneka and Prentice could enter the chateau. They went to the doors of the great room and Roma hesitated before opening them. "Just a heads up that Randall was here this morning. He dropped off another series of paintings." Machaneka was trying to remember if Odara had asked him for more artwork as Roma opened the heavy door for them. When she and Prentice stepped into the room she was mesmerized.

A series of five paintings, all the same size, were leaning up against the wall nearest the fireplace. Each of them had a full moon in the background. The first one was of Machaneka standing in front of the Sacred Council, holding the hand of Odara when she was a little girl. The second one was of Machaneka in an embrace with McKenzie and Lizzie in the forest. The third picture was of the elder Odara lying in bed looking out of the window at the full moon. The fourth picture was of Prentice handing Machaneka the cord of fire with the moon glowing above them. The fifth picture was just a moonlit sky, nothing else. The fifth picture was unfinished. She and Prentice marveled at the details in every picture. The facial expressions and body language that Randall had captured so accurately, it would have been hard to believe that he hadn't been on their journey with them. Machaneka's eyes went back to the picture of the elder Odara, and she decided to excuse herself so that she could channel her. She didn't want to just show up for a visit to heal her and give her a heart attack in the process.

Machaneka asked Prentice to excuse her. He sat down in one of the large wing back chairs and told her to go ahead. "Remember, that you cannot make a wrong decision, Machaneka."

She smiled at him. "I know." She walked out of the great room and headed towards her prayer room. Mutora having served Phillip his tea, was heading in her direction as she took to the stairs. "Before you go upstairs, there's something that you should know."

Machaneka kept walking up the stairs. "You can share with me in a little while, Mutora. Right now I need to attend to something in my prayer room."

Mutora raised her voice so that Machaneka would understand the seriousness of her request. "Make sure that you speak with me before you do anything else when you leave out of your prayer room!" Machaneka stopped in her tracks. Mutora had never raised her voice at her.

"I promise, Mutora." She walked down the hall to the small room at the end of the wing.

The prayer room was just as she had remembered when she was last there as Odara praying for guidance. A small royal blue velvet chaise. A small light blue chair. An altar with white candles and incense. A royal blue, light blue, silver and white prayer rug in the middle of the floor with pillows around it in various shades of blue, and a portrait of Odara wearing a navy-blue evening gown hung on the wall. Machaneka took off her shoes, lit the candles and the incense, and lay down on the super soft chaise. She closed her eyes and visualized Elder Odara, and she kept that visual in her head. She began to feel as if she was in the room with the elder. And then she saw her clearly, sleeping with a peaceful look on her face. Machaneka sensed a presence and scanned the room. Sudan was asleep in a rocking chair by the window.

She had grown into a beautiful young woman. Machaneka fondly remembered the little girl with the big brown eyes who had sent her a call of distress when her mother was in danger. She turned her attention back to the elder. She did appear to be quite frail, and Machaneka noticed that the color in her skin had an undertone of gray in it. The elder lay in the bed in very pretty, yellow pajamas and was bundled up quite nicely for warmth. Sudan's family had been taking good care of her while she was ill.

The elder stirred in her sleep and then opened her eyes. She greeted Machaneka with a smile. "I knew you would be here sooner or later."

Machaneka wished she were physically there to hold her hand. "Of course I would, I just need you to hold on through the night. Tomorrow I will be there to help you. I have some healing tools that can pull you through this. You don't have to succumb to this." To Machaneka's surprise, the elder shook her head and then responded to her.

"No, you will do no such a thing. I am ill, but I have passed the point of suffering. I am not interested in being here any longer. I had an amazing life and you made it even more amazing by assuming my younger body. There is plenty of me left for this place in her. It is my wish that you tend to her and make sure that she is stronger than ever when I leave here. My job in this capacity is done. Promise me that you will honor and respect my wishes to relinquish this shell that I reside in."

Machaneka was fighting back tears."I promise, Elder Odara, to honor your wishes." The elder raised herself up slightly in her bed and then spoke again. "Make the decision that makes you feel good about who you are deep down inside. Deeper than even who the Sacred Council knows you to be. Everything will work out best if you honor yourself.

Until we meet again, Machaneka." The elder blew her a kiss and Machaneka blew one back to her. She pulled herself out of the state of channel and sat up on the chaise. Her heart was aching, she needed to lay eyes on her beloved Odara. The problem was that the bedroom had been sealed and she was not supposed to see her until she presented her decision to the Sacred Council and or reassumed Odara's body. She reclined back onto the chaise and tried to relax her mind while she figured out what to do next. As she stared out of the window into the night from the chaise, she was moved to stand as the full moon filled the sky, brilliantly orange in color in a cloudless sky. Machaneka took a deep breath, lay back down on the chaise, and as she closed her eyes she said, "The fifth moon."

When the sunrays came shining through the window in the prayer room, the warmth of them on her skin awakened her. She had fallen asleep fully dressed and everyone had just let her rest. She opened the window to take in the fresh morning air, and a large orange and black butterfly landed on the windowsill. She greeted the butterfly and then sat on the prayer rug to pray. She was just rising to her feet when Mutora and Roma came and entered the room. She knew from the look on their faces that the elder had passed away overnight. Machaneka sat back down for a moment and Mutora and Roma put their arms around her. She allowed them to comfort her as she sat in silence.

During the evening, Phillip had returned to the realm of the universe where the Sacred Council resided. When he arrived, the Council was abuzz with conversation and wonder. The elder Odara had relinquished her body and was currently moving through the realm of transition. Isis summoned Phillip to speak with him. "In lieu of the current circumstances we have lifted the seal to Odara's bedroom. Machaneka will need to see her in order to have some peace about the elder Odara's transition. We're concerned about her ability to make a clear decision in light of what has happened.

For more than one reason, we allowed Shaju entrance to Odara's bed chamber before Machaneka returned from the containment realm. The issue is that he refuses to leave before he speaks with Machaneka. We had almost convinced him to leave but now that the elder has died he will surely not move until he speaks with her." Phillip looked at the goddess Isis and asked how problematic that could prove to be.

She leaned forward on her throne. "Extremely, especially since Prentice will take issue with the conversation that Shaju wants to have with her.From here we watch every move and listen to everyword until Machaneka joins us to give share to the decision that she has made. We must be prepared to intervene if necessary."

Phillip nodded at Isis. "Very well! I am all ears and eyes until she arrives."

Mutora and Roma had left Machaneka alone to process and think about what to do next. She wanted to ask Prentice what she should do but instead she got up from where she was seated and left the prayer room, headed to the opposite end of the hallway where Odara's bedroom was. Even if the room was sealed, she could at least get close to the door and sit by it.

She remembered that Mutora had something to tell her, but she decided to get to that when she made her way back downstairs. Machaneka approached the bedroom cautiously. She didn't want anything else to have to explain to the Sacred Council about breaking rules. When she got to the bedroom, she was shocked to see that the door was ajar. Realizing that the seal had to have been broken, she rushed into the room in a panic thinking something had happened to Odara.

When she entered the room, she stopped in mid step. "Shaju!" she screamed and ran to him. Shaju was sitting on the side of the bed looking over Odara's body when Machaneka had entered the room. He stood immediately and swooped Machaneka up in his massive arms. She buried her head into his chest and began to cry.

"What are you doing here? Tell me she's not gone!" Machaneka was speaking while sobbing.

Shaju wrapped her up even closer to him. "I heard about your journey and the reason for it and needed to speak to you. No, she's not gone but early this morning her body went into a state of distress. I've been watching her closely." Machaneka pulled away from Shaju and went to Odara's bedside. The color in her skin had faded some and her breathing was labored. She was almost despondent for a moment and then she pulled herself together. Machaneka pulled the small box that Trevelyn had given her out of one of the folds in her robe. Then she retrieved the sash that she had tucked into her dress. While she had been on Mount Huayna Picchu, she had used some of the gold thread from the hem of her gown to make the headpiece and body chain with the stones that Trevelyn had given her. She took the jewelry out of the box and placed the headpiece on Odara's head and forehead. Then she tied the other piece around Odara's neck. She made sure to pull the piece all the way out so that the jade stones were in alignment with Odara's seven chakras. Shaju stood back and watched patiently as Machaneka opened the sash and took out the flower petal. She gently lifted Odara's head and placed the petal underneath her pillow. Once she did that, she shook the pollen from the flower into her hand. Carefully and slowly, she shook the sash over her open palm until there was no more pollen left in it.

Machaneka anointed Odara's head, hands, and feet with the pollen and then placed her hands above her heart chakra. Machaneka slowly moved her hands above Odara's body from head to toe and then back again. The heat from Machaneka's palms was causing Odara to begin to sweat but after a few minutes her breathing began to relax. Machaneka worked Odara's entire body relentlessly and she felt when Odara's body began to respond to her healing. She heard her heart begin to beat strongly. She saw the color returning to her skin and she saw the look of pain leave her face. Machaneka did not stop for hours. When she finally relinquished her hold on Odara, she was exhausted, and Odara was lying in the bed brilliantly illuminated.

Machaneka turned to Shaju. "She only needs to rest now and so do I," she said. Shaju exited the bedroom with her and then asked if they could speak before she went to rest. "Of course, beloved, let's go into the library." Machaneka then led him to a room just a few steps away.

As Machaneka and Shaju were headed into the library, Prentice had just been made aware of the elder Odara's passing, Odara's body being in distress, and that the seal to the bedroom where Odara lay had been removed. He immediately excused himself from Mutora and Roma and went upstairs to check on Machaneka. Certain that she was probably with Odara, he set out for the bedroom. Halfway down the hall he stopped when he heard a male voice coming from one of the rooms. Prentice walked to the door of the library to see what was going on. The first thing that he noticed was that Machaneka looked exhausted; she was listening intently to Shaju! Prentice wasn't pleased to see her looking so tired and he didn't like that she looked like she was torn in two. When he heard what Shaju was saying to her he understood why she looked that way. Shaju was trying to convince her that what they had was not at a complete loss. If she accepted full ascension, they would be side by side fighting for the greater good of the universe and would be together forever. He told her if she did not accept that, he would lose the only chance to have her for a second time.

Machaneka's head was reeling. The events of the last few weeks, the elder dying, Odara being in distress along with Shaju trying to convince her to make a decision in this instant and go to the Sacred Council was almost too much. She told him she would do nothing in haste. Then with a burst of energy from a painful memory she addressed him loudly. "You have always had my heart, but I would like for you to remember that there was a time when you could've chosen to be with me or ascend. You chose to ascend. I hear you, and I love you dearly, but I will not be coerced to make a decision that I am not ready to make. Thank you for keeping watch over Odara but please go now, Shaju. I cannot- I will not deal with anything else until I know that Odara has fully healed, and I have rested and can make a sound decision."

Shaju was about to respond to what she said when Prentice spoke up. "You have been asked to leave so that Machaneka can rest. Please honor her wishes." Shaju flew to the door and was face to face with Prentice. The elusive, legendary Prentice that he had almost attributed to folklore. Before he could tell Prentice that this was none of his business, Prentice spoke again. "Absolutely, Machaneka is my business. I have been assigned to accompany and protect her and I will do that, regardless of from whom or what. Please do not try to engage in a power play, it is unnecessary and unproductive – not to mention you will lose. Leave her be, Shaju. She will reach out to you once she has rested." Shaju and

Prentice were face to face, nose to nose, and the thought of them fighting was frightening and overwhelming.

"Shaju, please!" Machaneka pleaded. He hesitated and then stepped back. "I am leaving now. Remember us, Machaneka." Then he looked at Prentice. He had resigned himself to leave but not before sizing up the being that he knew in his heart was in love with the woman that he had loved forever. Prentice saw in Shaju's eyes that he knew. He didn't care that he knew what Machaneka did not. He only cared that he left so that she could rest. Shaju raised his wings and spread out his arms and was gone. Machaneka walked past Prentice out of the library and closed the door behind them. She took two steps and then began to collapse. Prentice caught her before she hit the floor and carried her into the bedroom next to the library.

Machaneka had only exhausted herself that way one time before, and Prentice had been there that time to take care of her the same way that he was now. When she awoke the next afternoon having slept through the night and the morning, she felt somewhat rejuvenated. Mutora was bringing in breakfast and humming a tune while Roma drew the curtains back with a smile.

Machaneka asked what everyone was so cheery about. Roma came over to the bed. "Prentice has been on constant watch alternating between you and Odara since yesterday. He is quite the spectacle in his devotion to the both of you. The events of the day before came flooding back through Machaneka's mind. She couldn't believe that Shaju was going to try and challenge Prentice, or that he was so selfish that he insisted that she decide immediately. That left a bad taste in her mouth. She still loved him, but she was realizing that it was not the same as before. With that thought still in her head, Prentice stood in the doorway to the bedroom.

"May I come in?"

Machaneka sat up in the bed. "Of course you may." Prentice came in and sat down at the small table by the window. "While you were asleep, I continued the bodywork that you started on Odara. She is regenerating and healing quite nicely. How are you feeling?"

Machaneka took a bite of her toast and responded with a mouthful. "I feel great. If I only spend the next week or so resting and overseeing Odara, I'll be better than ever. I don't want anything else to happen. I don't want to do anything else or go anywhere else, and I don't want to hear any more bad news while I'm recharging for my visit to the Sacred Council." Prentice laughed and looked at her with her hair all over her head, a mouth full of toast, and her pajamas buttoned wrongly because he couldn't see all the buttons when he put her to bed.

"If it is peace you request, it is peace that you shall have. I will see to it." He wanted to ask her if she had made a decision, but he refused to submit to his curiosity after the pressure that Shaju had put her under. Machaneka sipped her tea and then stretched back out and began to drift back to sleep. She wanted to be sure that she was rested because she still had healing work to do for Odara. As she closed her eyes, Mutora and Roma cleared the dishes and began pushing the rolling cart back out of the room. Prentice stood to follow them and let Machaneka sleep.

Mutora put her hand on his chest. "You stay, she needs you and doesn't know it yet." We can take care of everything else." Prentice saw the seriousness in Mutora's eyes and deducted that he would not win an argument with her, at least not this one, so he moved from the seat at the table to the reclined chair by the bed and sat back down.

Roma looked at him and said, "Thank you, and you are correct, that is an argument you would lose." Mutora and Roma left the room and Prentice took off his shoes and settled into the comfortable chair that faced Machaneka.

8
The Decision

Machaneka turned over in the bed after sleeping for several hours. She saw that she was in the room alone and got up to go check on Odara. She walked down the hall to Odara's bedroom and saw Prentice in the room leaning over Odara. She stepped closer into the doorway and watched as he moved his hands above her body transferring energy. He moved slowly and deliberately, not taking his eyes off Odara even though he knew that Machaneka was watching him. She did not interrupt him. Her heart swelled watching him take such care of her beloved Odara's body. When he stopped, he turned to her and said, "She is as strong as an ox."

"Thank you. I am rested enough to continue the rest of her healing work."

"That may be so, but the decline of the full moon is upon us, and I needed to make sure that when that sun rises after the decline that she is strong enough to hold you when you reassume her body as you were instructed by the Sacred Council. That, and I didn't want you to have to reassume her body and then heal it from the inside. So much had happened that Machaneka had forgotten she was to reassume Odara's body so soon. She was confident in Prentice's ability to do the same healing work that she would've done and probably even be better at it. She was grateful that he had the foresight to think to maintain it. Now recalling what the Sacred Council ordered when they visited, this was the last day before reassuming Odara's body and then thirty days to make her decision. On the thirty-first day, Phillip would be back to get her answer. She thanked Prentice again for everything and then remembered to thank him for speaking up for her when Shaju was being relentless. He accepted her thanks and then said, "I can see why you love him so deeply; he is absolutely fearless. If it makes you feel any better, I would not have hurt him. I just would've let him know that it was a no-win situation for him."

Machaneka smiled and told him that she knew that. As she walked away to go downstairs and walk around the chateau, she looked back at him and said, "Loved him."

The next morning Machaneka rose early to find Prentice asleep in the chair next to her bed. He looked like an angel even in his sleep. She walked into the hallway and Mutora and Roma were standing in front of Odara's bedroom excitedly. She smiled at them and gave both of them a hug. They embraced for a minute and then Machaneka went into the bedroom and closed the door. Prentice was awakened by the sound of the door closing and he arose to see where Machaneka was. When he walked into the hall and looked in the direction of Odara's bedroom he saw Mutora and Roma standing guard in front of the closed bedroom door. They were quite the pair looking so innocent, kind and sweet, but he knew that if he dared try to enter that room before Machaneka reassumed Odara's body, there was no telling what spells and mayhem would break out. Just as Machaneka was certain that there was so much more to Prentice that she did not know, he was certain of the same where Mutora and Roma were concerned.

Machaneka walked over to the bed and looked down at her beloved Odara. She was flooded with the warmth of love as she placed her one hand on Odara's womb and the other over her heart. Machaneka waited until she could feel the rhythm of Odara's heart and the flow in her womb simultaneously. When she felt it she spoke aloud, "Receive me!" Odara's body quivered and then relaxed. She opened her eyes and looked around the room. The last thing that she remembered was that she had to be placed in a state of rest. She looked at her into her palms and studied them for a moment. Five months had passed. She was slightly disoriented and then she felt a quickening inside of her as Machaneka settled fully into her body. Odara got out of the bed and looked in the mirror. She was pleased to see that her rest had not affected her physically. As a matter of fact, she noted that she looked and felt stronger. She went to her closet and pulled a fire red kimono from the closet. Then she changed from the robe that she had been at rest in. After looking at herself in the mirror and admiring the jade body chain that hung from her neck sparkling with diamonds and sapphires, Odara opened the bedroom door to go find Prentice.

Odara did not have to take more than a step out of the bedroom to see Prentice. He was standing adjacent to the door next to Mutora and Roma who were still in front of the door. The three of them all gasped at the sight of her standing there. Not because they hadn't expected her to eventually come out of the room but because everything about her appearance was electrifying. Prentice quickly gathered his composure and said to her, "It's time to eat! Mutora and Roma have a feast fit for a queen downstairs."

"By all means, I am famished," Odara quickly replied. "Five months of spirit food only leaves a girl pretty hungry." They all laughed and headed downstairs to the dining room.

The meal was indeed fitting for a queen; quail, beef wellington, fresh roasted vegetables and potatoes, spiced shrimp, salad, caramelized peach tarts and wine and coffee. Afterwards, Odara and Prentice went outside to her orchard for a walk in the early afternoon sun. They stopped at a bench under a plum tree and sat down. Prentice took Odara's hand and they talked for hours about everything they could think of. Time passed quickly and the sun was beginning to set. Odara looked at Prentice and said, "I have thirty days."

"They will fly by if we spend them all like this," Prentice responded. And that is exactly what they did. After breakfast every day they were inseparable.

They took day trips into the city, exploring shops, local pubs, and farmers markets. They rode out for hours across the countryside in her carriage to have lunch in fields and under trees. They spent almost every moment of every day for the next twenty-nine days learning and enjoying one another.

On the eve of the twenty-ninth day, Prentice appeared at Odara's bedroom door and asked to come in. She welcomed him and he began to speak. "No matter what you have decided, I will remain by your side. I will repeat for you that with everything that I have and am, I will protect you as your companion and friend. I will also do so because after thousands of years I have finally had the opportunity to experience the feeling that you call love. I will never leave you, Odara, and if your body should expire, I will continue with you in the next." Odara was speechless. "If I had known that all I had to do to get you to be quiet was to tell you that I love you, I would've told you sooner." Then he put his arms around her and kissed her. He released her and then turned and walked away. She wanted to tell him how she felt but she couldn't open her mouth.

Prentice turned back to look at her and said, "I already know, beloved, the words aren't necessary." Odara sat on her bed and undressed slowly. In the morning Phillip would arrive to get a decision from her. She put on her nightgown and got in the bed. She tried to sleep but kept tossing and turning. Getting out of the bed she opened her door to find Prentice about to open it. He stepped inside and closed the door. They got into her bed and Odara curled up on his chest with his arms around her. In less than five minutes she was in a deep sleep.

The sound of birds singing with the sunrise awakened Odara. She rose from the bed and went to shower. She let the hot water from the shower run over her from head to toe as she lathered herself in a soap fragranced with Egyptian musk oil. When she exited the shower, she went to her closet and chose an emerald green long flowing dress that she loved. After dressing and combing her hair out fully, she pulled her hair back from her face and put on a gold headband and a gold amulet around her neck. Satisfied with what she saw in the mirror, she spoke to herself. "It's a great day to deliver a decision." When she walked out of her dressing room, Prentice had also left her bedroom. She felt amazing as she headed downstairs for a cup of coffee. She figured Phillip would be there about noon, and she would be ready to greet him once again as Odara.

She made her way to the patio adjacent to the kitchen for coffee and Prentice was already there enjoying a cup. He stood and pulled her chair out. They sat and shared idle conversation holding hands and drinking coffee. They had just decided to go for a walk on the property when the doorbell rang. Odara was not nervous at all. She had made a decision that she was comfortable with, and she was ready to deliver it. She and Prentice stood up from the table and she began walking towards the great room where Phillip would be waiting for her.

Prentice sat back down to await her return. It mattered not to him what her decision was, he was going to support it and be by her side.

Odara entered the great room and Phillip was, as usual, impeccably dressed. In all white from hat to shoe. It was quite stunning on him and Odara was tickled to see that he had returned to his more formal self. Phillip was secretly ecstatic on the inside to see Odara again. He never told Machaneka that he too was quite fond of her. He embraced her quickly and then asked, "Have you come to a decision, Odara?"

She took a moment and then responded. "Yes, I have. I have decided to decline the promotion to full ascension. I am aware that although I can still be promoted to higher sentry rank, I will never again be offered to assume full ascension. I will continue to serve the Sacred Council with the same loyalty and devotion as before. My decision has been well thought out and is final, Phillip." Deep down Phillip was thrilled. If Odara had ascended fully, there would no longer be a need for them to interact.

He took Odara by the hand. "Very well then. I have a message for you that was to be delivered in the event that you declined full ascension. After I relay your decision to the Sacred Council, some of whom will be greatly shocked and others highly impressed, you will have a period of rest. When that period of rest concludes, you will be summoned by the council for your next well-deserved promotion. Isis in particular is quite pleased with the way that you handled yourself throughout your journey. She has decided to overlook your acceptance of a gift from Jerifenn due to the unfortunate nature of circumstances where that gift ended up being a critical part of your healing. I shall be on my way now." Phillip embraced her again and then left the room. Odara was a bit taken aback. *Another promotion – even after I declined full ascension.* She hurried out of the room to tell Prentice.

When Odara went to rejoin Prentice on the patio, he had moved to a bench in the shade by her rose bushes. She walked over to him, and he saw in her eyes what her decision had been. She shared the conversation that she had with Phillip and then she exhaled. Prentice listened and then exhaled as well. "What would you like to do now, Odara?"

She looked up at the sun and said, "Maybe some traveling during this 'period of rest,' not local though. I'd like for you to take me places that you loved being. Aside from my journey to make a decision, I've never been able to explore the universe without an assignment, Prentice."

Prentice sat up straight. "We can begin our travels tomorrow. I know exactly where to begin."

They both sat back and Odara put her head on his shoulder. "I'm looking forward to it," she said. They were both excited and enjoying the afternoon sun in the quiet beauty of the rose garden and Odara was completely at peace. After a while they decided to go inside because Odara wanted him to see her Sacred Garden that could only be entered from the door that led to outside in her bedroom. As they were walking up the stairs, they both stopped all motion at the same time. The sound of tribal drums in the distance hit their ears and then began to get closer and louder. They both knew what those drums meant; Odara was about to get another assignment. Prentice had a look of disbelief on his face and Odara just shook her head. "So much for a period of rest," she said. She wasn't bothered at all by the disruption of their plans. Odara was at her peak, and she was prepared and ready for anything.

Mutora and Roma had returned to their assumed positions as Giselle and Nicolette. Now that Odara was her full self again, they had gone back to the normal formalities of maintaining a chateau. The weather was beautiful, and she set about opening windows throughout the home to allow the fresh air to flow through. Nicolette was in the kitchen prepping the ingredients for the night's eveningmeal and thinking about how everything had just settled back to normal in the blink of an eye. She stopped what she was doing and stepped out into thepatio to have a glass of water. While she was drinking her water and enjoying the view of the orchard in full bloom, she thought she heard the voice of Prentice. Nicolette turned around but didn'tsee him. Thinking that he must be in the kitchen with Odara she returned to enjoying her view. Then she heard his voice again. "The sound of sacred drums has returned. I do believe that soon we will beleaving you again for another assignment." This time Nicolette turned around and saw a black

Persian cat perched on the top stair of the walkway to the orchard. Prentice who had assumed the form in which he was assigned to Odara, was stretching and purring enjoying the afternoon sun. Nicolette laughed aloud.

"I almost thought I was losing it for a moment. I forgot that you are so many things, Prentice. Hopefully the drums were just a welcome home for Odara."

Prentice stared ahead out over the orchard and then curled up on the step. "I hope so. The thought of it sent Odara into preparation mode. She's in her Sacred Garden tending to her herbs, and then she said she was going to go into her pantry and see if anything introduces itself to her. She was particularly excited about opening her chest to see what may have been added to it. As for me, I just want to enjoy the sun and tour the grounds. There's so much ground that I can cover quickly in this form."

Nicolette smiled at him. She was grateful for his presence. "Well then, have a great tour and enjoy. I'll call for you when dinner is ready. Should I set out a cat dish or will you join Odara at the table?" Nicolette giggled as she was walked back into the house. Prentice smirked at Nicolette as she walked away laughing, and he slowly started walking down the steps into the yard that led to the orchard.

Odara sat on the end of her bed thinking about the time that she had spent thus far as a spirit warrior for the Sacred Council. She was humbled by what she had accomplished. As she had moved from body to body, she had never taken inventory of her work or assignments. Now, after her spirit form Machaneka reassumed her body, she had been given another gift. Every experience that Machaneka had before she became Odara was part of Odara's memory. It was in her fiber like they had become one and it was as exhilarating as it was overwhelming. She was honored to be where she was and have the companionship of someone as powerful as Prentice.

She decided that she would gather some herbs from her Sacred Garden and take a long hot bath. Bathing was a full ritual and self-love experience for her. She was thinking to get some lavender, chamomile, eucalyptus, and most definitely rose petals from one of her rose bushes. But before she did that, she wanted to open her chest and see what may have been added to it by the Sacred Council.

Odara went into the room that also held her secret pantry to open the large cedar chest that was in the corner. The trunk was made for her by a master craftsman who only made things from wood, metal, or stone at the request of the Sacred Council. The chest was indestructible and had been created for the sole purpose of containing ceremonial robing, gifts from the ancestral realm, and protective wear for engagements with adverse forces. When she first received it over a thousand years ago it only held one robe and a staff. Now it was almost full of ornately-covered robes, belts, jewelry, and other artifacts created by humans but infused by blessings and energies from the spirit world to assist her. She knelt in front of it to speak one of the incantations that had to be used along with the key to open the trunk. There were different incantations for different purposes and needs. The key without the right words wouldn't work and the words without the key wouldn't either.

A side panel of the chest had been configured so that the key was a part of the design, and it would only reveal itself for her to access after the incantation. "Me, Us, We, call on you, Ultimate Mother/Father God, for access to that which is needed to fulfill our purpose once again. We ask for spiritual food in the form of strength. We seek guidance, we humbly request that you reveal what will be of assistance and accept that what you present is divinely presented with grace for the greatest of all good. Wehallate, shohalik, tonatidis-mishobetah, uncalitodia – Nosephta. Yahseh."

After a few moments, a light began to emanate from the right side of the trunk and the key raised from the design. The trunk had one other special attribute besides needing a key and proper incantations to open. If the Sacred Council received a request for assistance and did not feel that you would require any, it simply would not respond to your efforts. Odara had bid it open more than once before and nothing happened. This was to ensure that you did not become dependent on the council and to make sure that you understood that most of the time you as a spirit warrior are already equipped with everything you needed to complete your assignments. When it did open, however, whatever you had been assigned to do may need the assistance of something blessed by someone older and stronger than you.

She removed the key and opened the lock. Lifting the lid carefully, Odara braced herself for whatever had risen to the top of its contents for her to utilize in her next assignment. She made a thankful note to self that she never had to dig through its contents and try to figure out for herself what she might need since she never knew what exactly may take place during a battle or if there would be one. The trunk would rearrange its content on its own, bringing to the top in plain sight what the council had decided you may need. Everything else would remain folded and bound so that you knew that it was not necessary nor to be disturbed for the current assignment.

With the trunk now open, Odara stared at what was sitting on top. She was so unprepared for what she saw that she stepped back from the chest and closed her eyes. After a few moments she opened her eyes and stepped back in front of it. Sitting on top of the contents of the trunk, were a set of small wings and an amulet that held a fire opal encased ingold. As she was staring in disbelief, wondering what the wings were for, the wings began to flutter lightly. The longer she stood staring, they began to flutter with more vigor. It took her a minute to understand that she was supposed to take them out of the trunk. She had gone to look into the trunk to simply see what she had been gifted for whatever assignment was next. Now she was clear that this time, she wasn't supposed to wait for the assignment. Odara reached into the trunk and gently lifted the wings. As soon as she had them in her hands free from the trunk, the opal in the amulet still inside of the trunk began to glow a radiant red. The wings began to flutter again, and her palms began to heat up. She wasn't sure what was happening until the wings spread apart and flew up to the ceiling. In less than a moment, the wings flapped a couple of times and disappeared.

Odara was confused about what had just happened but attributed it to a message that would later reveal itself. She picked up the beautiful amulet that was still glowing and radiating and secured it by the gold chain that it hung from around her head. The fire opal hung perfectly in the center of her forehead, and she was about to grab a mirror to see what it looked like adorning her crown when a wave of heat rushed over her from head to toe and she was rendered motionless and unable to speak.

Odara felt a small sense of panic; something was happening that was foreign to her and she could neither move nor cry out. Her rapidly growing fear was causing the temperature in the room to rise, and she saw the candles on her table begin to melt. Then she felt her back straighten like she was being forced into a vice. At the same time her mouth opened, and she felt herself begin to rise from the floor off her feet. She heard the sound of wings flapping softly. She raised her hands to command her body back to the floor and that is when she felt the muscles in her back moving. Her voice returned to her, and she let out a loud joyous laugh. Odara was flying. She had been gifted her first set of wings from the Sacred Council. She couldn't believe it. She was not unaccustomed to traveling through the air, but she had never done it with wings. Excitedly, she flew from corner to corner in the room, to the top of the vaulted ceiling and then did it over again. She lowered herself and removed the amulet and her wings folded away. She hurriedly closed the trunk and ran out of the room. She could not wait to show Prentice.

Prentice had been in the orchards and moving about the full property that the chateau sat on for hours when he felt and heard Odara cry out. He broke into a full sprint, changing from Persian cat to a full-grown panther so that he could get to her quickly. He stopped in his tracks when he got in view of the chateau. From where he stopped, he looked up and realized that her cry was not distress, it was joy and laughter. That realization was quickly followed by a full view of the window to the room where Odara kept her trunk. Through that window, Prentice watched from the outside as Odara flew back and forth past the window with a full set of wings! He was relieved, amused, and proud. Obviously, the Sacred Council had big plans for her regardless of her declining her promotion. As he reassumed the form of a black Persian cat, he began slowly walking towards the chateau. He knew that Odara would be looking for him in her excitement to share her greatest gift from the council yet. Taking his time, he wondered what their next journey together would be as he again heard the sound of tribal drums far off in the distance.

*We're always one decision away
from a completely different life*

Booking & Contact Information

Erica Harrison

Talent Agent/Booking Mgmt.

Harrison-Brownlee Innovation

502.264.2853

erica@harrisoninnovation.com